T0294808

Managing Previously Unmanaged Collections

Managing Previously Unmanaged Collections

A Practical Guide for Museums

Angela Kipp

ROWMAN & LITTLEFIELD
Lanham • Boulder • New York • London

Published by Rowman & Littlefield
A wholly owned subsidiary of The Rowman & Littlefield Publishing Group, Inc.
4501 Forbes Boulevard, Suite 200, Lanham, Maryland 20706
www.rowman.com

Unit A, Whitacre Mews, 26-34 Stannary Street, London SE11 4AB

British Library Cataloguing in Publication Information Available

Library of Congress Cataloging-in-Publication Data

Names: Kipp, Angela, 1977- author.
Title: Managing previously unmanaged collections : a practical guide for
    museums / Angela Kipp.
Description: Lanham : Rowman & Littlefield Education, 2016. | Includes
    bibliographical references and index.
Identifiers: LCCN 2016011926 (print) | LCCN 2016012998 (ebook) | ISBN
    9781442263475 (cloth : alk. paper) | ISBN 9781442263482 (pbk. : alk.
    paper) | ISBN 9781442263499 (electronic)
Subjects: LCSH: Museums—Planning—Handbooks, manuals, etc. |
    Museums—Collection management—Handbooks, manuals, etc.
Classification: LCC AM121 .K55 2016 (print) | LCC AM121 (ebook) | DDC
    069/.068—dc23

LC record available at http://lccn.loc.gov/2016011926

∞™ The paper used in this publication meets the minimum requirements of
American National Standard for Information Sciences—Permanence of Paper
for Printed Library Materials, ANSI/NISO Z39.48-1992.

Printed in the United States of America

This book is dedicated to all museum professionals who do their work unnoticed, out of the public eye, knowing that while no one will ever know their name, it is due to them that history is preserved.

Contents

Foreword

In a perfect museum universe, this book wouldn't be necessary. All of the objects in every museum collection would be completely documented. Each would have a fully visible number physically attached to it, a corresponding paper file full of information about its provenance and use, and a record in an electronic database that included all the relevant description that would make it possible to identify the object with the touch of a button. And of course, the location of the object would be accurate and always up-to-date.

Unfortunately, few of us who work with museum collections live in that universe. More often, descriptive or provenance information is missing, the object number is unreadable or absent, or the location hasn't been checked or updated for several years. When this is the case for only a part of an otherwise documented collection, or when there is only a small backlog of objects that need attention, this is generally considered to be part of the registrar or collections manager's daily work. In those situations, this book wouldn't be necessary either.

However, there are times when a huge new acquisition is made and there is little or no descriptive information, no lists of what is in each box or on each shelf, or even what is in the collection as a whole. Other times an older museum without a professionally trained collections staff has continued to collect without cataloguing what they already have. A registrar or collections manager is hired and, in addition to all the other daily responsibilities, there are storage rooms full of unnumbered objects, now separated from any acquisition information, to be dealt with. In both these situations, the collections must be processed, inventoried, and assessed for relevance to the museum's mission and exhibition needs.

These situations are not just backlogs, but Projects with a capital P (not to mention Problems with a capital P). Often either the collection gets ignored for as long as possible, preferably until someone else takes over the job, or it brings the daily collections work to a complete halt. Now this book is necessary.

There are few, if any, guides on how to approach unmanaged collections. As the author makes clear, much of the traditional, item-by-item, way of thinking about museum objects doesn't work when faced with the size and scope of these collections. The "best practices" kind of detailed description only gets in the way when dealing with large groups of unsorted, undocumented objects. Putting the emphasis on the "big picture," sorting on a large scale, and limiting the kinds of descriptive information that is gathered, are only a few of the key innovative approaches advocated here.

Also important is the recognition that there are always limited resources available for this kind of work—whether they are time, money or manpower. Reaching out to the wider community for practical help in the form of materials and labor, as well as background information about the collection and its history, is a critical factor in having the necessary tools to reach a successful conclusion. Equally important is identifying the emotional support that one's colleagues bring, both in celebrating successes and in offering sympathy when plans don't work out or need revising.

But perhaps the most important new idea in the approach put forward here is that of "logical exits." Creating order from apparent chaos takes time and energy. Even if an outside collections expert is hired to do the job, there will be many times that the size of the collection will make the work that needs to be done run well beyond the amount of funding available. And for a museum collection staff that tries to fit the work into a break in their daily tasks, even if it is scheduled for a time when the museum is closed or less busy, there will always be interruptions. To know when it is logical to stop work for a while, write up your progress, and take care of other responsibilities, is a powerful tool.

Whether your title is registrar, collections manager, or museum technician, one of the most important parts of your job is to make the museum's objects accessible, both physically and intellectually. To put it simply, this means that you are responsible for knowing what you have and where it is. And, whether or not it fits within your daily schedule, fixing a large, previously unmanaged collection is "your mess now." *Managing Previously Unmanaged Collections: A Practical Guide for Museums* will make sure that you know how to do what is necessary.

Janice Klein
Executive Director
Museum Association of Arizona

Preface

"I was taken to a shipping container holding facility. . . . All the artefacts were stuffed into the container and I knew straight away there [would] be some casualties. My jaw was agape and I was wondering what I had just gotten myself into."[1]

A painful situation—and one no museum studies course or material-handling training will ever prepare you for. You landed a job to take care of a collection and instead of working in a nice, clean, HVAC-controlled storage area you are standing in a small dusty shed someone has declared to be the future storage of the soon-to-be-opened local museum. The objects are not stored in a nice shelving system but are literally piled on the floor. Or you are confronted with a room that is filled floor to ceiling with unmarked boxes and it is assumed you will "make this collection accessible" within a given time frame. An unpleasant, yet not uncommon, situation for a museum professional.

Too many collections are neglected because the people in charge don't have knowledge about collections care, don't know where to start, or wait until a large sum from a grant comes in. When upper management finally calls a museum professional to the rescue, that museum professional will find a situation that is far from best practice. In order to make these collections accessible for research and exhibitions, one has to choose an approach that is very different from the one learned at university or the one developed when working in a larger, well-ordered, and managed collection. The situation resembles more an emergency response than the usual collection management practice. As the museum professional responsible for organizing this collection, quite logically you have to adapt a working style that resembles a first responder to a disaster or a doctor on the battlefield more than a collections manager working with his or her collection.

This book was conceived for the reader who is confronted for the first time with an unmanaged collection. It is not a do-it-yourself guide to collections management as that knowledge comes only with years of training, continual professional development, and last but not least, a lot of practical experience. It was written as a guide to lay out the work that needs to be done, but more importantly, to understand how to see that work as a progressive task. Those with many years of experience might find this book refreshing for its information as it reminds one how little details affect the bigger picture; and to not lose sight of what comprises the bigger picture and its surroundings. It is written by a practitioner in the field for the active or prospective practitioner in the field. The language is kept simple and figurative not in an attempt to dumb down but because that is the way the author likes to speak and illustrate things when actually working with real colleagues in the real world of museum collections.

Given the experiences of the author, the main focus is on historical collections and those collections with a science, technology, farming, and/or history background. Other collections might need a slightly different approach. It's written with a completely unorganized collection in mind, in a situation where no collection management or documentation procedure of any kind is in place. But some of the procedures described will be helpful as well when transferring a large collection with thousands of objects into an existing museum collection.

In general, every situation is different and every collection is different. What might work in one setting may not work in another. This book does not present the final answers to every question. Think of it as a road map. It contains a general path to follow and known dangers and issues, but, to stay with the image of a road map, if you discover a river that is not mapped, you have to look for a raft or a bridge by yourself, meaning that you will have to find solutions that work in your setting—and maybe solutions you have not read about in any book. The aim is to encourage you to do so, to find your own ways and get creative in preserving the collection. It shows ways to approach a worst-case scenario in logical steps. Each step keeps in mind that you will be most certainly limited in money, time, and staff, and shows what can be achieved toward improving the collection in spite of these facts.

There will be "logical exits" at the end of some of these chapters. Those are points at which you will have the collection in a condition that allows you to leave it for the next lucky person to take over. A common issue is that time frames are often so tight that the target of having the collection in good shape at the end of a contract or at a fixed date can't be met. Another scenario may be that other projects become more important and you have to stop working on the collection, which might sound familiar to many directors of small museums. "Logical exits" are the points at which you can stop without risking that everything you've done so far or since the last "logical exit" was a waste of time. For contractors, those "logical exits" might serve as orientation points when negotiating the work that has to be done on the collection.

Managing Previously Unmanaged Collections: A Practical Guide for Museums is based on a lot of real-life experience, working in the field and exchanging thoughts with registrars, collections managers and other museum professionals around the world. To illustrate why some things are important, every now and then you will find a real-world example in the text that illustrates some of the issues mentioned in this chapter. This is not about pointing the finger at someone, it's about lessons learned—often the hard way. In the last chapter you will find even more real-world examples of managing unmanaged collections. I'm eternally grateful to all those colleagues who stepped up and told their stories. Some of those examples are really close to the worst case. They may serve as a motivational read—the situation you, the reader, is confronted with might not be as bad. If it is, it illustrates that others were confronted with similar issues and survived to tell the story.

This book presents basically a logical sequence of steps one has to take to bring order into the chaos of a previously unmanaged collection. Woven into this sequence are chapters with some special aspects that are important for keeping the whole project on track. Those chapters are:

1. "Congratulations, It's Your Mess Now." This chapter introduces the mindset you need to approach a previously unmanaged collection. Especially if you recently graduated from a museum studies course or were working for a larger, reputable museum, you might have to adapt from looking for the best solution to looking for solutions that work with what you've got. It's also a chapter about the responsibilities and hardships that come with taking care of a collection.

2. "A First Glimpse" is about how to approach the new collection when you see it for the first time. It's a first analysis of issues and potential dangers that is, maybe surprisingly enough, a hands-off approach.

3. "Back at the Desk." Now that you have an idea of what and where the main issues are, it's time to pull all information on the collection together and organize it in an accessible way. This chapter is about securing what you already have, as well as determining what you will need. At the end of this chapter is the first logical exit: a documentation of the current state of the collection and a plan for the next steps.

4. "Getting Organized" is the first step where you will actually work with the collection itself. It's about setting up a working space, putting in place the most important security measures, and getting the most urgent maintenance issues done. The logical exit here is having the storage area brought to a safe stage—both for the objects and for the people working with it.

5. "Diving into the Collection." This chapter is about bringing the whole collection into a structured form so the actual accessioning and cataloging can take place. This means sorting the objects into logical groups and getting rid of items that don't match the collections policy. The logical exit is to have a collection that is ordered into groups or categories that can be tackled by the next person or team taking over.

6. "The Power of Coffee" is about the human aspects of a collections management project. Basically, this is about networking, about connecting with other museum professionals, but also about reaching out to town officials, police, firefighters, and the community in general. Last but not least, this chapter talks about the cooperation with interns, volunteers, and veterans.

7. "Getting Stuff Done" is about exactly this. It helps you to develop two strategies: a documentation strategy and a collections care strategy. The documentation strategy lays out a sequence of steps for accessioning and cataloging the collection, while the collection care strategy prioritizes what should be done in terms of preventive conservation. When both strategies are developed, they have to be interlinked to an overarching plan. With this chapter you reach the point where you have to define the next logical exits all by yourself in relation to your plan. While moving forward in documenting the collection you define tasks that can be done as soon as there's money, material, and/or an expert for it.

8. "Storage Wants and Storage Needs" considers storage organization. It helps you develop a master plan of how your storage should look in the future and helps you to develop a storage improvement strategy on its basis. It discusses common issues like space estimation, storage layout, storage furniture, containers, and location numbering. In the end it takes a look at the most common mistakes when it comes to storage organization.

9. "We Had Nothing" is about sourcing money and materials. Finding and applying for grants is a way to get money, but it's not the only one. This is a chapter about creativity. Collaboration with other museums in buying materials, public events to raise money for the collection, presenting on the web an object desperately in need for conservation. The possibilities are nearly unlimited for a creative collections manager.

10. "Failing Successfully" is about failures, failures that aren't failures, and the importance of embracing one's own mistakes, as they give you the chance to analyze what went wrong and make improvements. You can't make an omelet without breaking eggs and you can't work on a collection without making mistakes.

11. "Success Stories." Despite the overwhelming feeling that managing unmanaged collections is a Sisyphean labor, one that can never be accomplished no matter how hard you try, there is a lot that can be done. In this chapter you

will find a few real-world examples of previously unmanaged collections and what was done to improve the situation.

In the Bibliography you will find a selection of publications that might be helpful, as well as some professional resources and communities on the web.

And now, without further ado, let us start managing an unmanaged collection.

NOTES

1. Antony Aristovoulo, "Match-Ball for the Registrar!," *Registrar Trek Blog*, April 5, 2013, http://world.museumsprojekte.de/?p=1141.

Acknowledgments

This book would have not been possible without the input of many friends and colleagues in the field. It was their joint experience and wisdom, their willingness to share and discuss that shaped and enriched the rough idea for a book project I outlined in autumn 2014 to Charles Harmon, executive editor at Rowman & Littlefield.

From the very start I was surprised by the overall support for this project by the professional community, especially in the United States. Whoever I told what I was planning to do thought it was a good idea and encouraged me to write it. Maybe the first one I told about it outside of my family was my friend Darlene Bialowski, principal of Darlene Bialowski Art Services, a former chair of the Registrars Committee of the American Alliance of Museums, and a person who has seen a great many unmanaged collections. She volunteered to read every chapter, suggest edits, and point me to sentences and paragraphs that were not as clear and easy to understand as I wished they were. More than that, she was the guiding spirit of the project, always willing to answer my sometimes-difficult-to-answer definition questions and discuss my conundrums. I'm deeply indebted to her and until this day I seriously don't know how she managed to cram all this into her already tight schedule.

Then, I feel very honored that Janice Klein, Executive Director of the Museum Association of Arizona, agreed to write the foreword and supported the project with her thoughts and advice stemming from years of working with small museums.

Susan Maltby, conservator at Maltby & Associates, Inc. in Toronto, read the manuscript upon completion and helped refine it with many practical ideas and thoughts. Paul N. Pallansch of Up-Close Realism, Silver Spring, Maryland, a friend and builder of amazingly compelling dioramas, provided the so-much-needed view of someone not directly involved with collections care, making sure it was easy to understand for an "outsider."

This project would be pointless without the real-world examples and the pictures. It was amazing to see how many colleagues were willing to share their experiences and waive license fees for the good cause. I would like to thank Ashley Burke (Burke Museum Services, LLC), Mary Helen Dellinger (City of Manassas Museum System, Virginia), Jodi Evans (State Historical Museum of Iowa), Christina Johnson (FIDM Museum & Library, Los Angeles), Bruce MacLeish (Curator Emeritus of Newport Restoration Foundation), Susanne Nickel (Eskilstuna stadsmuseum, Sweden), Maria Scherrers (Adidas Archives, Herzogenaurach, Germany), Alicia Woods (Washington State Parks and Recreation Commission), and Elizabeth Wylie (Flannery O'Connor – Andalusia Foundation, Georgia) for writing down their real-world experiences and Andrew Goldstein (Valdez Museum & Historical Archive, Alaska), Susanne Granlund (Eskilstuna stadsmuseum, Sweden), Meghan Grossman Hansen (FIDM Museum & Library, Los Angeles), Regina Menclik (TECHNOSEUM, Mannheim, Germany), Katherine Owens (Missouri State Museum, Missouri State Parks), and Angela Stanford (Museum of Danish America, Elk Horn, Iowa) for providing this project with beautiful pictures.

This project was supported by the readership of the Registrar Trek Blog. During the writing process I often discussed special issues there and got feedback that proved extremely helpful in writing certain chapters. It would be unfair to name some contributors by name here, because I'm sure I would forget someone and it would neglect that it often were "likes" and "retweets" on social media that encouraged me to keep on writing. So, I just say, "Thank you all!"

I would like to thank the team of the TECHNOSEUM for the great time I have had there since 1998, for the many things I've learned, for those I'm still learning, and for the laughs. Again, it would be unfair to throw around names. Especially as it is the whole staff and its will to work professionally—to provide the best service possible and to overcome obstacles—that makes me feel proud to be part of this museum.

I would not have been able to write this book if my parents hadn't supported my unusual career choice—and I guess it is due to my father's passion for country music that English never felt like a foreign language to me.

Last but not least, I want to thank Bernd Kießling, my colleague, friend, counselor, critic and—most important—significant other, both for actively discussing the topics of this book with me and for keeping me grounded by patiently taking care of household and cats while I was writing in the evenings and on weekends.

List of Abbreviations

AAM—American Alliance of Museums
AASLH—American Association for State and Local History
CMS—Collections Management System
DIY—Do It Yourself
HEPA—High-efficiency particulate arrestance. HEPA air filters are crucial in vacuum cleaners used in a collections environment.
HVAC—heat, ventilation and air conditioning
ICCROM—International Centre for the Study of the Preservation and Restoration of Cultural Property
MRM5—Buck, Rebecca A. and Jean Allmann Gilmore. Museum Registration Methods. 5th ed. Washington, D.C.: The AAM Press, 2010. It is such an important framework that you will often encounter the term "MRM5" in professional conversation and correspondence.
NPS—National Park Services
PDF—Portable Document Format
PE—Polyethylene. Many archival packaging is made of PE, but not all PE is archival; it depends on the additives the manufacturer uses.
RCAAM—Registrars Committee of the American Alliance of Museums
UNESCO—United Nations Educational, Scientific and Cultural Organization

Chapter One

Congratulations, It's *Your* Mess Now!

It might seem funny to you that the first chapter of this book is not about starting to work but about developing a certain mindset. But it is important because tackling an unmanaged collection needs a different approach than what you will find in books or learn in courses about collections care and preventive conservation. These books and courses always have the well-managed collection in mind. But with an unmanaged collection that should either be managed as a whole or included into an existing collection, you are faced with challenges that are different from those of a well-organized collection. If you have already worked in a well-organized museum some of the things you have learned so far and served you well might stand in your way when you are confronted with an unmanaged collection. If you have this background, some of the things recommended here might seem counterintuitive at first. However, be assured that they are written to create the foundation for working according to best practice in collections care some day in the future. To adjust your mindset to work with an unmanaged collection, there are three principles you have to take to heart:

1. Think of the whole collection, not of single objects.
2. You are a collections manager, now think like a project manager.
3. See the big picture, work in small steps.

Along with these three principles there exist three dangers you should strive to avoid:

1. Don't be spellbound by numbers.
2. You are not the white knight.
3. You are not a collections management machine.

Figure 1.1.   Storage view of the Landesmuseum für Technik und Arbeit in Mannheim, December 1991, TECHNOSEUM, Foto Klaus Luginsland

When you have taken those dos and don'ts to heart, start off with the mantra for your project: "This is my collection now and no matter what happens, I will bring it to a better state."

Think of the Whole Collection, Not of Single Objects

This principle might be the hardest to learn, especially for the experienced collections professional, because it goes against everything one has learned and most certainly against the natural feelings of someone who has taken up the job as a museum professional because of the love for old things. In addition, all formal training is aimed at having one single object and deciding on how to treat it properly and finding the right packing, climate, and storage condition. So, how can this thinking possibly be problematic?

If you approach a large number of objects, you might naturally spot one object that is in desperate need of treatment: a fragile wooden box under a plow, a glass vial crammed between heavy objects, a crinkled certificate in a dress . . . . Your immediate thought is to go and save it. But this might not be the best approach. While caring for this single object, you might have overlooked some more serious issues. You might have destroyed a connection to the other objects in the vicinity by taking it out. Or you might have simply lost precious time because this object is either damaged beyond repair or is not of any significance to the collection. By doing the right thing in principle, you've done a disservice to the whole collection.

To understand this concept better, think of a doctor being called to major railway accident with many injured persons: while this doctor has the formal training and certainly the inner desire to help the most severely wounded first, he can't do that. He has to do what is known as "triage." He has to decide a sequence on who is treated first and who can wait; his aim is to save as many as possible with his limited resources. He also can't just go in there and start treating the injured. His medical knowledge is needed to do this triage, while other first responders can take up the immediate treatment of the injured, as instructed by him. He has to decide who to treat first and how. This sometimes means deciding someone doesn't get the intense treatment that might be necessary to save this single life. The resources are needed to save the lives of many others who have a higher chance of survival if they get sufficient treatment fast.

The good news is that no one will die because you set the wrong priorities when working with your collection. The bad news is that you are most certainly as limited in time and resources as the doctor at the accident. So, in the broader perspective, wrong decisions result in treating fewer objects the right way and therefore do harm to the collection as a whole.

As a side note, triage is known as one of the most stressful tasks for civilian and military health personnel. Many need psychological help after such an assignment. Make sure you have a good support group and colleagues to reach out to who would understand your situation. Read chapter 6, "The Power of Coffee," for more.

You Are a Collections Manager, Now Think Like a Project Manager

Note: If you are a freelance museum professional or a long-term director of a small museum you can skip this part, because you already do this.

As a collections manager your concern is the well-being of the collection. This goes without saying. But in many large and mid-size museums, that's where your responsibility ends. You'll have other people who are responsible for accounting, human resources, marketing, and so forth. In a small museum with an unmanaged collection, you don't have those additional resources. Needless to say, those tasks have to be done just as well and the only one who can do them is you. If your task is to merge an unmanaged collection into an existing one, you are in a similar situation: those resources might be there, somewhere in your museum, but someone needs to tap them in favor of the unmanaged collection. Yes, this someone is you.

You will need money, time, and presumably staff to do the work and if you don't calculate and act like a project manager, it will be very difficult to persuade your director, the board, the development department, your community, or whoever is responsible to provide you with the necessary resources. So, even if you have never done this, you have to lay out a schedule—a plan with needed materials and tools and a budget. And you have to keep track of your plans as you progress and adapt them to reality. Always think of the citation that is credited to Dwight D. Eisenhower: "Plans are worthless, but planning is everything."[1]

But being a project manager is more than making plans and following them. It's also about seeing the logical steps that need to be taken to succeed. It is about seeing, way ahead of every other person involved, potential issues that could occur along the path and solving them before they become problematic. It is about spotting opportunities and using them in favor of the collection. It is about assigning tasks to people who are able and willing to do them and about supervising so they are done properly.

If you are an experienced collections professional, this adaption in mindset might be even harder to do than the shifting of focus from the single object to the whole collection . You have probably chosen the path of collections management because you like working with objects better than doing marketing, accounting, or managing people. But you have to learn and own these tasks now, in favor of your collection.

Probably you are used to doing everything on your own without any help. The latter can be a big advantage in the process but you have to adapt, because you won't be able to manage an unmanaged collection all by yourself. You will need help from other people in different forms. Volunteers helping with documentation, donors bringing in objects and money, service companies providing knowledge—there is a great deal of collaboration and teamwork involved, even if you don't have a team at all.

The hardest part is to let go of certain tasks when you find someone who is able and willing to do them. If you found a volunteer who is a natural in object photography, it's time to let him or her do it. It's your task as a project manager to make sure this volunteer has all the materials for the work. Sure you have to keep an eye on the process and help with questions, but avoid being on this volunteer's back. You have delegated the task, now let him or her do it.

The key is to understand that you are steering this project. No matter where you are in the hierarchy of a larger institution or what your position is in the big picture of a small community, you are responsible for this collection. You are taking it from the unmanaged state it is in to a better condition. Don't let anything or anyone push you in the wrong direction, hold you back, or hasten your actions.

See the Big Picture, Work in Small Steps

In the first part of this chapter we talked about letting go of the focus on the single object and refocusing on the collection as a whole. But it's equally important to break your work down into tasks that are actually manageable. This book is written in the same manner—it shows you a general sequence of logical steps. But even within those steps it will be necessary to break the overwhelming responsibility into smaller steps.

This is especially important as there will be a lot of pushbacks and things not going the way they were planned. You will encounter resistance when you ask for resources. If you are part of a city's infrastructure, the city council might raise their eyebrows when you are asking for the roof to be repaired and tell you that they hired you to catalog the collection, not to care for the building. The same resistance may come from upper management or boards—however your institution governance is structured. Your applications for grants will be rejected. The community will vote for refurbishing the local swimming pool instead of repairing the museum building. This is resistance you have to cope with. It helps tremendously if you know the next step to take after such a backlash. Fine, you might not have been granted the money to fix the roof, but you can start with sorting the collection, for example. It is extremely important to just keep moving.

Make sure to set yourself realistic goals. "Sort the collection" is too big a task to perform in a single week or even a month. To keep yourself motivated you need smaller, achievable goals. "Sorting Box 1-3," "Phone Mr. Miller to talk about what to do about the moth infestation," and "Send schedule to volunteers" are examples for small steps on a to-do list—steps that are manageable and keep the process moving. Crossing things off a list is highly motivating and gives a sense of accomplishment. Make sure that there is at least one task on your to-do list that you can cross off at the end of the day.

Don't Be Spellbound by Numbers

When you are working with the collection it is important to remind yourself that you are there to improve the collection. It is not as important how many objects are actually cataloged but that the collection is stored safely and that you are able to hand it over to someone else in a better condition than before.

The sheer number of objects sometimes makes it tempting to set unrealistic goals for yourself. It holds also the danger of losing focus on what is important to do and what can wait a little longer. For example, if you are under a time-defined contract, it seems logical to divide the days left on the contract by the estimated number of objects. Quite logically, you get a number of objects that have to be cataloged each day. Although compelling, this is a very dangerous thing to do. The number you get leaves out of focus that cataloging the collection is just one of the tasks you perform. It leaves out buying materials, writing grant applications, researching pest treatment, talking to upper management and experts, managing volunteers, and so forth. As a result, you are haunted by a number that has nothing to do with your actual work.

It is a strange thing how we are spellbound by numbers. When working with an unmanaged collection you will have total strangers ask you how many objects the collection holds and how many objects one can catalog in a day. Worse, upper management might have a clear estimate of how many objects you can document in a day and keep nagging you about how many you have cataloged in the last month. It is important not to fall for this way of thinking yourself. It's easy to be occupied by a once-calculated number, feeling like a king when you outperform your own average and devastated when not reaching half of it, losing the rational knowledge that a number is just a number, a counting aid, nothing more.

A number says nothing about how good you are actually managing the collection. You can reach your calculated fifteen cataloged objects each day and leave your contract with an impressive 3,750 objects in the database and still, in the big picture, it is a failure because you have done nothing about the mold in the collection room, the water still comes through the hole in the roof, and half of the collection is damaged beyond repair because of the desperate storage situation. You can have a mere 100 objects in the database but because you have researched all necessary background information, cleared the legal status, fixed the roof, and improved the storage situation you are able to hand over a collection that will be in good shape for the future.

It is equally important to educate everybody who asks about numbers about this fact, as well as to keep yourself from overestimating numbers and underestimating the other issues.

You Are Not the White Knight

Having a vision, a picture of what we do and what we are, is a good thing—even sometimes necessary to do the job we do. I referred to the doctor at the railroad accident earlier and I've heard a lot of other useful images other collections specialists use: volunteer firefighter, surgeon on the battlefield, attorney for the artifacts, and so forth. However, there is one very dangerous self-impression: the noble white knight fighting for his collection.

Why is it so dangerous? A white knight fights for the good and against evil powers. Don't get me wrong; I'm totally okay with seeing mold and pests as evil powers that have to be fought and destroyed. But there is the danger of seeing everybody who doesn't do what you expect them to do as evil powers. And a white knight is very limited in his abilities; the only thing he can do is fight and he will either win or lose a battle. There is no in-between, no chance of negotiating and reaching compromises. If you don't get what you want as a white knight, you leave the battlefield beaten and wounded, and you take it personally. This helps neither you, nor the collection, nor any other person involved.

Instead of the white knight, it might be more helpful to think as an athlete or trainer of a football team. If a game is lost, it doesn't mean the whole season is lost. If you don't make it into national competition this season, there's always a next season. Just as every good trainer, you analyze why a certain approach failed and then try again and try it a different way. You don't retreat in anger when you are rejected; you focus on a different task until you have an idea what to try next. You find a different person to ask, a different source for money, a different solution to the problem. Whatever you do, you will come back and will come back stronger and with better ideas.

You Are Not a Collections Management Machine

As whoever you see yourself—doctor, surgeon, firefighter, athlete or trainer—you are human. This means you make mistakes (read chapter 10, "Failing Successfully," for more), you don't have superpowers and you are not invulnerable. Everyone knows that in theory, but in the working process you might forget about it.

Keep in mind that it is you, the healthy collections manager, who makes logical decisions based on thorough research and due diligence. It is you who is responsible, for taking that previously unmanaged collection and turning it into a well-managed collection. Your physical and psychological health is the foundation of your work. Neglecting it means doing a disservice to your collection. What it takes to keep oneself healthy is a very personal matter but I discovered that there are at least two points that apply to every human being: take all necessary precautions when working with hazardous materials and make sure you have a reasonable balance between your working life and family and friends.

THE MANTRA

When starting to work with a previously unmanaged collection you'll discover a lot of things that are not right, objects that are neglected, things done in an irrational way without giving any thought. In short: you have to deal with a mess. It's totally okay to curse a little bit when you start, but limit it to the first few days.

Whatever was done by those who worked on this collection before you, it doesn't matter anymore. Things might have gone wrong in the past, but from the very moment you take over, there is no excuse. You are responsible for this collection, so no moaning over what has been done wrong and no cursing your predecessors. Whatever you do, keep in mind that it's *your* mess now.

You have a vision: This collection's situation will improve over what it is now. In fact, it should become a best-practice, well-organized collection somewhere in the future. For this, it might help to have a mantra in case you discover something bad. It can be something like, "This is my collection now and no matter what happens, I will put it in better shape." I myself borrowed mine from a former boss and mentor: "It's alright. I'm a trained professional. I can handle this." Alicia Woods, Curator of Collections at the Washington State Parks and Recreation Commission uses, "As long as we take no steps backward—I can keep moving forward."[2] I have another colleague who hasn't a mantra, but whistles a certain tune. Pick any mantra you like, but make sure it is a positive, forward-thinking one. Then, whenever you discover something really bad, something done by someone in the past who seems to have had his or her brain turned off, you can take a deep breath and murmur your mantra (or whistle your tune).

Now, it's time to take a deep breath as you prepare to meet your collection the first time.

NOTES

1. In fact, Eisenhower said it in a speech to the National Defense Executive Reserve Conference in Washington, D.C., on November 14, 1957, but indicated that it is a much older saying. The full citation is, "I tell this story to illustrate the truth of the statement I heard long ago in the Army: Plans are worthless, but planning is everything. There is a very great distinction because when you are planning for an emergency you must start with this one thing: the very definition of "emergency" is that it is unexpected, therefore it is not going to happen the way you are planning." Dwight D. Eisenhower, *Public Papers of the Presidents of the United States, Dwight D. Eisenhower, 1957* (Washington, DC: National Archives and Records Service, Government Printing Office, 1958), p. 818.

2. Alicia Woods in an e-mail to the author on March 30, 2015.

Chapter Two

A First Glimpse

If you ever searched for an apartment or a house you are familiar with this phenomenon: While you are drawn to certain details like the beautiful view from the balcony, you miss other details like the mold in one corner in the kitchen. And your memory might play tricks on you: it might fool you on the color of the tiles in the bathroom or, indeed, tell you the window is on the left while it is on the right. In many regards, inspecting a collection for the first time is very similar. You might be drawn to certain objects and get carried away by your own professional self. As a collections care professional, you are trained to spot issues with objects, and because of that focus you might miss larger issues with the surroundings or the building itself.

That's why it is important to remember the shortcomings of your brain and work against them when you assess the collection the first time. You know what you do when you do a house viewing: you bring a good friend with you, take a lot of pictures and force yourselves to look for places with issues. With an unmanaged collection, you should take a very similar approach.

PREPARATION

Your task in this first step is to gain an overview, and this means taking pictures and notes. It doesn't make sense to recommend how to do this technically, for this is a matter of personal preferences. Some might prefer their smartphone; some, a laptop with different spreadsheets for different steps and issues; and some, pen and paper. Personally, I go with a new, pocket-sized notebook, a pencil, and a digital camera. Generally, it's not important how you do it; the only important thing is that these tools are working during the whole process. Things to consider:

- All batteries should be fully charged.
- Preferably, you have a set of extra batteries for all electronic devices.
- Never rely on there being electricity; everything you need should work without an outlet.
- Never rely on a working Internet connection or mobile reception, have all the information you need available offline.
- When working with a digital camera, have a set of new or empty memory cards with you.
- When working with an analog camera, have more film with you.[1]
- Never rely on just one pen; have at least three working ones with you. Pencils are preferable as they will work in every climate and on uneven surfaces, won't run out of ink, and are generally safer when working with collections.
- When working with a pencil, have an eraser and a sharpener with you as well as several backup pencils; or use a mechanical pencil.

You will have to assess the condition of the entire place where the collection is stored. As you will never know what to expect, consider that this might include climbing on roofs, wading in mud, or crawling through shrubbery. While I don't recommend that you bring all your outdoor equipment, the following things have proved to be useful more than once:

- a tape measure (of course, a laser rangefinder is even better, if you have one)
- a variety of gloves[2]
- a good, bright flashlight (with a set of replacement batteries)
- a miner's lamp that you can wear on your head and allows you to use both hands
- ziplock bags in different sizes
- tweezers
- a multi-tool—a small device with various helpful tools like knife, pliers, screwdriver
- a device to measure temperature and humidity
- safety boots or at least sturdy shoes
- a jacket with a hood

Neither this list nor any of the following is exclusive. There is a whole lot of other stuff you might find useful, but this will be dependent on the collection you work with and the region you work in. To illustrate: a pair of rubber boots is very handy in a muddy boiler room of an industrial hall, but unnecessary ballast in a shed in the desert. Think about possible issues and equip yourself accordingly, thus developing your own equipment list.

When accessing the collection the first time, if you are lucky, you are guided by someone who already knows the collection. Take advantage of this and try to ask as many questions about the collection and the building as possible. This will be a bit difficult because at the same time you should not be distracted from the task of spotting potential issues. It is best to explain to this person beforehand what you will be doing on this first visit and why. This way he or she gets the idea and can become your second pair of eyes—pretty much like the good friend you take with you when visiting a potential new apartment, only that this friend will already know the apartment.

THE ISSUE-SPOTTING MODE

The most important thing in getting an overview is to work systematically. Some find it easier to start with the collection and then take a look at the storage room, the building, and its surroundings. Some prefer it the other way round. Both approaches work, as long as they are followed through systematically. Here, I will begin from the outside, working in toward the collection. I find it easier, because as a passionate collection manager I'm too easily distracted by objects as soon as I see them.

What follows are checklists of things to look out for while approaching the collection. It might be helpful to create your own that you can carry with you while assessing the collection. Where it seemed appropriate, there is a short explanation about why gathering this information is relevant. Most of the questions you can answer yourself, but for some you will need to ask someone who knows. The lists are nonexclusive. Some things might not be relevant in your special case, while other things that are utterly important might be missing.

Now put yourself into issue-spotting mode. It's not your task to admire the collection or the building; you are here to spot possible problems. Your goal is to gather all the information you need to develop a plan for the work in the next few months. This is the site where you will spend most of your time, so it's equally important to spot what building permanent fixtures are there (i.e., toilets, elevators, staircases) and if simple things like a desk and a chair are available. Keep in mind that some issues not only affect the collection, but they can also affect your health. For example, discovering mold is as important for you as it is for the collection. You have to develop a plan on how to deal with it and you will certainly need safety equipment for working with the collection. For this chapter, it's important only to discover all obvious issues. Taking action against them is part of the following chapters.

Taking a lot of pictures in this step is essential. Not only pictures of potential issues but also of the building and its rooms. You might not have spotted an issue right on-site, but if you took a picture of it you may discover it later. Pictures will make it easier for you to mentally go back to the place and help you to establish a plan for setting up a working area. Pictures will also be useful if you decide to call in an expert to review some issues later on. In short, there is no such thing as having taken too many pictures in this step; and with almost everyone using a digital camera these days, it costs you nothing.

It helps to decide beforehand how you will identify the places you take pictures of. If you have a map of the building the collection is stored in, you could already name or number different rooms and other locations (aisles, hallways, areas in the garden). Read chapter 4, "Getting Organized," for ideas of how to name locations. You can even create a file structure beforehand so it's easy to sort the pictures immediately after your visit. No matter if you do or don't know what to expect, you should remember to take notes on what you are photographing so you don't end up with a pile of photos and trying to recollect in which room they were taken.

Prepared and in issue-spotting mode, you are now ready to assess your new working environment. Next up are the checklists, working from the outside in.

Note: If you are just taking over a new collection that already is at a museum or other facility with appropriate collections-processing conditions, you can jump to the section "The Collection."

The Surroundings

- What is the infrastructure like? Is it easy to reach the building by public transport, car, or truck? This information is useful for a variety of reasons, including how easy or hard it will be for volunteers to come to work or if a truck-mounted crane will be able to make it to your place.
- Where is the closest fire department?
- Where is the closest police station?
- What facilities are in the vicinity? Make a list of firms, craftsmen, factories, and service providers. A roofer in the neighborhood is obviously helpful with a leaking roof. A nearby chemical factory might emit pollutants and you will have to check if they affect the building or can enter the building and potentially harm the collection.
- Where are the closest stores? While it is easy nowadays to order each and every thing via the Internet you might be in urgent need of a bunch of garbage bags, a handful of screws, or simply a sandwich every now and then.

- Consider the neighbors. While in larger museums you try to keep museum storage secret, with smaller institutions that's often a different story. Chances are that in a small community simply everyone *knows* that there is museum storage in a certain building. Therefore your next-door neighbors are as important for you as your security guards are in a larger museum. Put their names down and consider visiting them as an item on your to-do list.

The Building Outside

- Is there a fence around the building? What is its condition? Are there other security features (think small, this can be a gate or barbed wire)?
- Is the outside of the building clean or is it overgrown with bushes and vines? These themselves could be safety and pest issues, and the plants can conceal other issues with the walls.
- Are there any visible cracks, holes, or rotten parts?
- Do the walls feel dry or wet? Take a special close look at the foundation.
- How does the roof look? Are there visible holes or missing tiles?
- How does the drainage system look? Are there downspouts and gutters? Are there sewers in the street, close to the building? All facilities that contain water are often a source of issues if not properly maintained.
- Is the building level with the street? Higher? Lower? This is relevant both for potential danger of flooding and for accessibility.
- How large is the entrance door? How is it secured?
- How many entrances lead into the building? Take note of their width, height, and general accessibility.

The Building Inside

When entering the building it's extremely important to use all your senses. For thousands of years, we human beings were highly dependent on our senses, leading us to food and cautioning us against dangers. In our modern world we mainly use our eyes, but our other senses are still there and can tell us many things if we just pay attention to them.

Start with the smell when you enter the building. Older buildings will always have a certain smell from their furniture and the use of a lifetime, but there are certain smells that stick out. Mold has such a significant smell that we even use "moldy" as the adjective for it. Is it there? You will have to find the source. Urine has a prickly, sourish note and if you are trained you can even tell the difference between urine of mice, possums, and squirrels. To start with, if there is a smell of urine, you most certainly have a pest issue and one of your next steps will be searching for excreta to define what it is. If there is a smell of rotten meat you will have to search for a dead animal.

All of these smells point you to the fact that you most likely indeed have a variety of pest issues.

While these are all natural smells, search also for man-made smells. The most dangerous might be the smell of gas. I never heard of a museum professional killed by a gas explosion on the job, but leaking gas pipes and bottles are not uncommon. You should know the smell and if you recognize it in the building, avoid any sparks, get the heck out of there, and contact the closest fire department.

Most smells are not a hint to such severe issues. But a distinct chemical smell is alarming and you have to find out where it comes from. Maybe something in the building was treated for pests. Find out what it was, when it happened, and which chemicals were used. Maybe there are chemicals stored and something is leaking. Follow the smell and if you discover stored chemicals, take notes on whatever you find. Be very careful, and when in doubt, you had better leave and come back with a specialist. More harmless, food smells will point you either to food cooked and/or stored in the vicinity of the collection or a food processing firm nearby—both issues you will have to deal with.

Now it's time to use your other senses: What do you hear? A dripping sound can lead you to a leaking water pipe or a hole in the roof. Other noises can point you to issues with the heating or other technical facilities. Your skin will tell you much about temperature and humidity. While it's always safer to measure them, your skin can tell you things a device can't. A drop in temperature from one room to another can tell you to measure the temperature in both rooms where you otherwise would have just measured the temperature in the collections room. This can tell you that there is an issue in one of the rooms. A slight draft can point you to a window that doesn't seal properly or the fact that a wall is an exterior wall without insulation.

While we proceed with a checklist, always remember to use all your senses, not only your eyes.

- What is the floor made of? Is it concrete, brick, wood? What is its condition? Be especially careful in older buildings. You would not be the first museum professional finding him- or herself one story lower after walking on a brittle historical floor in the attic.
- If there is a carpet, is it an old one? You might want to check if it has a historical significance and if it is infested by carpet beetles or moths.
- How wide are the aisles?
- Is it possible to access the room with the collection at ground level? If it isn't possible, is there an elevator or just a staircase?
- Is it possible to reach the collection from the entrance with a cart or pallet jack if needed?
- Look at the walls. Are there cracks, holes, or wet spots?

- Look at the windows. Do they seal properly? Are they locked? Is it easy to open them from the outside?
- Where are the water and sewage pipes installed? Assessing their condition will be easiest if they are visible; if they are installed inside the walls you should research for plans in the next step.
- Are there toilets? Where are they situated? Are they operational (crucial for working at the building)? And where do the sewage pipes lead?
- Is there a kitchen? Is it in use and is there an exhaust fan? Where do the water and drainage pipes come from and where do they lead to? A kitchen is a potential danger as well as a much needed facility to get some warm water and take a break away from the objects.
- If there is no toilet and no kitchen, do you have access to these facilities nearby? If you haven't, this means that you can't work with the collection on-site and you then have a whole range of logistical issues to address.
- What about electricity? This is about two very different issues: First, deteriorated electric cables, outlets, and fuses are a potential life threat and fire hazard. Second, an old electrical installation might be unable to support all the devices you need for working with the collection. As you are most certainly not a trained electrician, try to connect with someone who can help you with these issues (read chapter 6, "The Power Of Coffee").
- Check out the heating system if there is one. How old is it? What's the fuel and where does it come from? Is there a backup in case it fails? It doesn't hurt to note the manufacturer, type, and serial number of the furnace or other heating system type.
- For the rare occasion where there are additional systems like HVAC, a fire suppression system, or a burglar alarm, make note of the manufacturer, type, and serial number, as well. If you find a contract number or manufacturer's number or a phone number of a maintenance company, note it.
- Find out if there is someone responsible for maintaining the facilities. Maybe there is a facility management service firm or some local craftsmen on contract.

There is a whole range of possible issues and some sound outright hilarious if you are not in the position to deal with them. For example, there was one museum where the sewage pipe from the main toilets went right under the ceiling of an archival room in the cellar; directly over the shelving units where historical manuscripts were stored without any further protection. In another venue, some cars were stored on the third floor without an elevator. The only way to get them out was through a waist-high large window. Surprisingly enough, no one remembered how they got there. In yet another case the building had a garden that was secured by a large gate with two locks and barbed wire. So far, so good, but on the backside of the building the fence had a large hole and empty bottles and cigarette stubs indicated that it was a popular meeting place for neighborhood youths.

THE COLLECTION

When you reach the room where the collection is stored, you will repeat most of the questions from the checklist you already used for the building inside. It's even more important at this point to use all your senses as described above, because all the issues you detect now are immediately affecting the objects. If you haven't so far, you will now want to take out your device to measure the relative humidity and the temperature in this room. In addition to the already used checklist, answer these questions:

- How is the collection stored? Is it on shelving units, boxes, or piled on the floor?
- What is the general condition of the room? Is it clean or dusty?
- If there are windows, how many are there? Where are they situated and does direct sunlight reach the objects? Is there a possibility to close the blinds?

Now try to gather all visible information about the collection. In this step, try not to touch the objects, even if it's difficult to refrain. Some items might have a connection to each other that is easily destroyed by moving them; some might be damaged because of poor storage, so they can literally break if you touch them. Last but not least, objects stored in piles can trigger a domino effect: if you touch one, another might fall and break. If the objects are stored in boxes you might have to open some of them, but be careful not to change the original order and don't rifle through them. Think of yourself as an ar-

A REAL-WORLD EXAMPLE

We called it the "Porcelain Palace." I can just see all of you nineteenth-century historians rubbing your hands, excited to hear about some great find of Victorian-era finery. The reality here is . . . no. Working for the Washington State Parks and Recreation Commission has taught me that life in a museum is The Life. Except for what was collected before you arrived in your position at a museum, you now hold the power to pick through a collection being offered—the power to pick the choicest of the choice. When you work for a land-owning, land-managing, public agency, the only power you wield is that over your gag reflex while maintaining a tight grip on your mission statement and hopefully an interpretive master plan. Sounds a bit extreme, but wait, let me place you in time and space.

In the late 1890s, the United States Army built Fort Worden, at the confluence of the Strait of Juan de Fuca and Puget Sound, in the town of Port Townsend, Washington. Along with two other forts, it protected the waterways leading to the urban centers and ports of western Washington. By World War II, the height of fort activity, there were at least 214 buildings and structures, not including the fortifications. Sometime before 1957, the property was transferred to the Port District of Port Townsend. At that time a considerable number of the remaining indigenous military objects were either repurposed, surplused, moved to forts still in operation, or stored in buildings at nearby federal properties. By the time the fort was turned over to State Parks in 1972, a lot, but not all, of the 214 historic structures remained in various states of repair.

In 2013, our Historic Preservation Officer, Stewardship Program Manager, and I were told the main campus of the fort was going to be managed by another entity and that we would need to assess the buildings for objects of historic value. The current use of a lot of the buildings varies, including vacation and/or retreat rentals, museums, a college, a print shop, and so forth. Some were used by park staff as equipment sheds and workshops, while others were used as offices and storage. We had heard we would see lots of refrigerators and electric range stoves standing by as replacements in the rentals. There were forewarnings of furniture in various states of repair, some authentic historic objects (but probably none indigenous to the era of planned interpretation), along with Army-issue, cast-iron cooking stoves, a search light tower (yes, the whole tower), a dinky steam locomotive (originally found buried on the property), and the Porcelain Palace.

The Porcelain Palace is a 30' × 60' building that is largely original construction. It was about one quarter full of varying generations of windows and doors and a quarter of it contained original cast-iron radiators. This left the remaining half an overwhelming mass of toilets and urinals spanning the decades from historic to contemporary—and clearly they had all been used. At this point you are probably wondering why. We were too, and have decided the most logical purpose (or the one we are telling ourselves) was for parts to fix toilets still in use.

The end result consisted of revisiting the interpretive master plan, while averting our eyes as much as possible. It was decided that while we didn't need any of these for current interpretive purposes, the possibility existed that some of the buildings associated with the fortifications could be rehabilitated for educational purposes. A representative sample was determined and we decided to leave the selection of that sample to the historians associated with the on-site museum, people who clearly had a desire to research toilets for this purpose. Eventually, I will number and catalog these, hopefully from a distance. Additionally, we retained a representative sample of the cast-iron radiators. The sample is a bit a larger than originally preferred because there were subtle variances of decorative reliefs on them, so it seemed logical to retain a sample of each. Our Historic Preservation Officer chose to retain all the original windows and doors. This will benefit restoration professionals since these can be used for producing replicas on appropriate historic structures, and some original glass and wood may be able to be retained to enhance the visual experience. Of course his biggest challenge will be to figure out which buildings a particular piece may have been associated with, since none of them were labeled.

The moral of the story: No matter what the object is (and in some cases no matter its condition), regardless of your first instinct during the triage process, you have to remember what your mission is and how it is associated with the mission of the institution you work for. Hopefully, you have a document or policy to guide you through this process. If you don't, build criteria and think ahead—many decades ahead. What are the possibilities or promises the property and object hold? What about the structures on that property? How will all of it benefit the public or scholarly research? Which elements fill those large details and which fill the small ones? What is the reality of human behavior and what objects fulfill the interpretation of real life needs? Think outside the museum and think about the overall potential interpretive environment both within and around the object. And always remember, no one wrote a book on how to triage used historic toilets—you are the author here, so stand tall, others may follow your example.

Alicia Woods, Curator of Collections
Washington State Parks and Recreation Commission, Olympia, Washington

Figure 2.1. The technology collection of the Eskilstuna stadsmuseum, Sweden in the unorganized state it was 2014 (Foto: Susanne Nickel, Eskilstuna stadsmuseum)

chaeologist who has to make sure he or she doesn't lose information because of digging too early and at the wrong place. As a rule of thumb: Take more photos, touch fewer things. This could be something like your own personal mantra to murmur while working with the collection.

One of the first steps you need to take prior to actually working with the collection is to determine what types of objects you have to deal with. Take note of general categories like farming equipment, household goods, clothing, and material groups like metal, wood, and textile. You will have to do a lot of research on storage and treatment for this collection, so you need to sort out what kind of information will be relevant for you. Spot potential dangers: furniture and textiles were often treated with toxic insecticides, taxidermy specimens were treated with arsenic, and technical equipment might contain asbestos. You might find it helpful to draw a small map of the storage room. This way you can mark the location of certain objects or spotted issues.

Next you will look for any visible issues. Dust, mold, pests, rust, bleaching. The possibilities are endless. You may want to take detailed pictures of issues like mold, as it is likely that you will need to consult an expert for treatment. If you find excreta or dead pests, collect them in ziplock bags and

Figure 2.2.   The same collection as in figure 2.1 after the first wave of reorganization 2015 (Foto: Susanne Granlund, Eskilstuna stadsmuseum)

write on them the location where each was found and what you assume it is. Use tweezers and/or nitrile gloves to avoid possible health risks.

To work on this collection, you will need to know approximately how many objects it contains. This is always the hardest part. Most certainly your first approach will be more of a ballpark figure than an exact number. You might easily be hundreds of objects off, but that's alright. You have to have an idea of what numbers you are talking about, so don't be shy. Try to find something that makes the estimation easier: if the collection is in shelving units, try to spot a shelf that seems to be a good representation of the collection with larger and smaller items alike. Count the number of artifacts on it and then multiply it by the number of shelves (if objects sit on the floor under shelving units, don't forget to count them as shelves!). If the collection is stored in boxes, try to find a representative box with not-too-delicate objects, empty it carefully—if possible without changing the original order—and count the items. Then multiply it by the number of boxes present. There might be boxes with just a few objects and some with many small objects, so they contain more items than a usual box. If you avoid those extremes, you will have a good sample box. For example: if your collection is the interior of a kitchen you might have a box with hundreds of spoons, forks, and knives, and boxes with just one or two cooking pots. If you search for a box with dishes and count its items you will most certainly get a good average number. The most difficult are collections that are just piled on the floor. You might take an approach of counting the items in a square foot and then multiply that number by the room size; but as piled collections are often quite varied in themselves, be prepared to be widely off the mark.

Last, you will have to work with the collection and this will raise the following questions:

- What about the lighting? Is it sufficient to work in the space or do you need additional lights?
- Is there a possibility of bringing in additional lights? Is there electricity at all, and if there is, are there enough outlets and do the fuses support them?
- Is there room for setting up a desk as a working place?
- Are there enough outlets for a computer and various other electric devices?
- If there isn't enough room for a desk, is there another room nearby where you could set up your working space?
- Is there a telephone or mobile phone reception?
- How about Internet? Is there a connection or the possibility to connect wirelessly via a nearby hotspot?
- Even if there isn't enough space for a desk, you will definitely need a space to set up a table or two to work on the objects and pack them. Where could you clear some space for that?

- Where is the closest source of warm water to wash your hands?
- Are there any helpful devices like ladders, carts, and/or a pallet jack? Your aim is to find out what equipment is already there and what will have to be bought or borrowed in order to work with the collection.

If you have come this far, you will have gathered a whole pile of notes and pictures. Your head will be filled with issues and you will feel exhausted. In the next step, it's time to go back to your desk and bring order out of the chaos of the gathered information. When you are done with it, you will see much more clearly what your next steps will be, so let's keep moving!

NOTES

1. Because the use of analog cameras is becoming more and more uncommon, I will from now on assume that you take your pictures with a digital camera or your mobile phone. If you work in analog, you have to adapt what is said about digital pictures to your analog copies.

2. Nitrile gloves are often the best solution, but not suitable for all objects and all occasions. For a good overview, read Claire S. Baker, "How to Select Gloves: An Overview for Collections Staff," *National Park Service Conserv O Gram* no. 1/12 (September 2010), http://www.nps.gov/museum/publications/conserveogram/01-12.pdf.

Chapter Three

Back at the Desk

What you've got now is a lot of information ordered in the least usable way: going from the outside in or the other way round. Next thing you need to do is to get an overview of what these notes tell you and work on your plan to tackle this collection. In order to do this you need one thing more than anything else: a quiet space with a desk that helps you to work on your strategy. Maybe there is a desk at the place where the collection is already stored or it is easy enough to locate some type of work surface to move into the space. But if not, you might need to work a few days from home or from the office of a friend.

ORDER THOSE NOTES AND COMPLETE THE INFORMATION

The things you noted are very varied, so you first have to find a way to organize them. The way you do that is up to you. Some like to create different word documents, others prefer to have a bulletin board or use file cards. Choose the method that works best for you.

There are four areas of information to be separated from each other:

1. basic information concerning the building in which the collection is stored,
2. basic information concerning the collection itself,
3. issues that have to be resolved, and
4. things you will need.

While separating those four you will discover additional information you will need and that you will have to research to complete your files and lists.

Basic Building Information

Basic building information includes all those door measurements, responsible tradesmen or service providers, telephone numbers, and so on. Those are things you should have quickly at hand when you need them. If the heating fails in the middle of winter, you should have the number of the maintenance firm at hand—no time for research and certainly not the time to compare different offers from different service providers. In this step of the process your task is to gather all the important information so you have it when you need it. Find out if the museum, historical society, community, or whoever you work for has contracts with craftsmen or firms for the maintenance of the building and technical equipment. If it has, take down all the important contact information in a way so that you have it at hand quickly. "Quickly" means that it is available wherever you need it and whenever you need it. In a file folder on your desk is fine, but also have it in your address book, mobile phone, and next to the respective device—for example, on a label with the phone number of the heating contractor in the room where the main heating system is. Make sure you are not the only one who knows where the important information is. Show it to everyone who might need it, for you might not be around when an emergency occurs.

In small institutions you sometimes will encounter "Paul." I use "Paul" as a pseudonym for "that guy/gal with the magical hands who can fix everything." Paul might not have a contract of any kind and might have no relationship with your collection whatsoever. It's just that it's Paul you always call in this town if there is something to fix because he has the skilled hands and the imagination to find practical solutions. Needless to say, you have to have his phone number in your contacts. And you should definitely meet Paul as soon as possible and explain what you are up to. Paul's ideas of fixing something might derive from areas of his life other than collections care. You might have to explain to him why epoxy isn't an appropriate solution for gluing a broken handle back to an ancient cup, for example. But as soon as he gets the idea of what collections care means, you might find a helper in all practical issues and conundrums you run into with your museum and your collection. Having said that, I know a few registrars and collections managers who became "Paul" in their museum or even in their community.

Try to find as much additional information about the building as possible. Plans are always useful and you should try to find at least a floor plan and a plan of the site. If it's not in the your institution's archive (if it has one), try the mayor's office, land registry office, or any other institution that is responsible for building administration. Your task is to collect all useful information, even if you don't need it immediately. If you find plans for water lines, sewage pipes, electricity lines, or whatever, they should go into your files. Same goes for instruction manuals of technical equipment.

Make sure you order all the collected information in a logical way and communicate it to everybody who might be concerned. It doesn't help if you are the only one who knows how you ordered the information and who is able to find the manual for the heating system or the floor plan. You should have at least one trusted person who knows where all the files are and how they are organized. This can be someone from the staff (if you are not the only staff member) or someone closely connected to the museum, like a trusted trustee. Be careful; there is a great possibility to shoot yourself in the foot: If a manual or plan was in a certain place for ages and many people know this, you should place a copy of this document there. In case of emergency, everybody will always look for it in the place where the document has always been, not in the new files.

Basic Collection Information

You have some notes concerning the nature of the collection. You know roughly what objects to expect and which materials to deal with. Now the research for relevant information begins. There are some books that should definitely sit on your desk, no matter what kind of collection you are dealing with:

Buck, Rebecca A., and Jean Allmann Gilmore. *Museum Registration Methods.* 5th ed. (MRM5). Washington DC: The AAM Press, 2010.

This is something like "The Bible" for every registrar and collections manager. It covers most aspects you will have to deal with and gives a good overview on current best practice in the field. You will often hear or read "MRM5" when someone refers to this book, because the fifth edition of Museum Registration Methods is such an important and often-cited framework.

National Park Services Museum Handbook, Parts I–III. Washington, DC: National Park Service, 1984ff.

You'll find the most up-to-date version on the website of the National Park Services (http://www.nps.gov/), where you can download it as a whole or in single chapters for free. Written originally for the collections in stewardship of the National Park Services, this handbook is continuously kept up-to-date with current research in collections care. It is structured as a series of questions and answers that make it easy to read and find relevant information quickly.

Dawson, Alex, and Susanna Hillhouse, eds. *SPECTRUM 4.0.* London: Collections Trust, 2011.

The *SPECTRUM* is the collection management standard in the United Kingdom and is widely accepted as best practice in other European countries. It covers most collections management issues and is available to download for free for registered users and non-commercial use at http://www.collectionstrust.org.uk/spectrum/spectrum-homepage. The standard itself is accompanied by other free collections management toolkits and resources.

Southeastern Registrars Association. *Basic Condition Reporting. A Handbook.* Lanham, MD: Rowman & Littlefield Publishers, 2015.

Although you will probably not have to do anything with condition reporting while working with an unmanaged collection, this book, with guidelines for handling and storing, is the most condensed overview on a wide range of material groups.

Reibel, Daniel B. *Registration Methods for the Small Museum.* Lanham, MD: AltaMira Press, 2008.
Catlin-Legutko, Cinnamon, and Stacy Klingler. *Stewardship: Collections and Historic Preservation.* Book 6, *Small Museum Toolkit.* Lanham, MD: AltaMira Press, 2012.

These two books focus especially on caring for collections of small museums, therefore they are more applicable to the situation of an unmanaged collection than books written with a large, well-organized collection in mind.

Malaro, Marie C., and Ildiko P. DeAngelis. *A Legal Primer on Managing Museum Collections.* Washington, DC: Smithsonian Books, 2012.

While working with the collection you will run into some legal questions and this book handles most of them.
There are many more good books concerning collections work. Perhaps the most concise overview of the last few years is *The Bookshelves User's Guide* by the Institute of Museum and Library Services, published in 2009, which recommends certain books for certain collection issues, along with a short content description and bibliographical reference. You can find it online on the website of the American Association for State and Local History: http://resource.aaslh.org/view/bookshelf-users-guide/.
Your further research for relevant books will focus on the special collection. You will need information concerning the preservation of the objects

in question, as well as information on the objects themselves for cataloging. What kind of information you will need will vary greatly, as it is dependent on the nature of the objects. It may include standard works of art history or indeed manufacturer's lists of tractors, vintage car magazines, or ancient mail-order catalogs. Make a list of desired literature and keep looking for opportunities to obtain them.

This list becomes part of the list of needed materials you will put together next. But never rely on getting money to buy those books. In fact, never rely on getting money for anything; you should always have another iron in the fire. In the case of professional literature: Spread the list widely and keep your eyes open. A community member's attic might hold old magazines and mail-order catalogs, long forgotten and not needed anymore, and the owner might be happy that they are useful to someone else. A larger museum in a neighboring city might be happy to find a good home for a previous issue of a book on collections care when it buys the new issue. A retiring colleague might want to get rid of his or her professional library.

The Internet is also a great resource if you know where to look. It's impossible to name all the good resources, so I'll go with the three websites I use very often:

- The Conserv-O-Grams of the National Park Service contain information on various material and storage issues: http://www.nps.gov/museum/publications/conserveogram/cons_toc.html.
- The Canadian Conservation Institute has very detailed notes on certain materials as well as very hands-on advice for preventive conservation: https://www.cci-icc.gc.ca/index-eng.aspx.
- Connecting to Collections is an online community that collects a wide variety of helpful information for collections care at http://www.connectingtocollections.org/all-topics/.

One of the dangers of the Internet is that you get a lot of search results that are not relevant for your situation, are not up-to-date, or are even false. Don't fruitlessly spend your time, especially not at this early stage of the project. In my experience it's best to start with a good overview and only dig deeper if special issues arise. And then, sometimes a phone call to an expert saves hours of research and cross-checking Internet information. Read chapter 6, "The Power Of Coffee," for more.

Getting an overview is your general aim. It is important to get a certain "feeling" for the objects you will be dealing with. This might sound a bit touchy-feely at first, but many veteran collections managers and conservators can tell you that this "feeling" is really important. This is especially true for the variety of objects that you will most likely encounter in small history museums. You will find many exact figures concerning relative humidity and temperature for different types of material in the guidelines for collections care, but those numbers often exclude each other. Metal should be kept at low humidity, wood at high humidity. Now, what to do with a chair made out of metal and wood? It is important to educate yourself about your objects, to get a feeling for why recommendations are made, what helps and what harms your objects, and why. When working with the collection you will need this knowledge to make the right decisions. The more you know by heart of what your object needs the easier it will be to make good decisions and the less frequently you have to check with the literature. Having said that, a good collections manager is always a curious and educated one. He or she will never stop keeping him- or herself up-to-date with the current research.

Along with the "feeling" for the stuff you are dealing with, you should develop a sense for dangerous materials in the scope of your collection. There is something like the "usual suspects" in collections care: arsenic on taxidermy specimen, pesticides in furniture, or asbestos in cinema projectors are well-known. But there might be other things that look innocent on the outside but contain danger: fire grenades are a good example for the kind of historical objects that are collected because they are "beautiful." They are, but they also contain carbon tetrachloride, which is a potential health risk[1]. Educate yourself on typical potential health risks with a certain group of materials. This includes ways to handle them safely and how to properly dispose of them if necessary. Of course, every kind of protective equipment for yourself and potential coworkers should go on the list of needed materials. The contact information for disposal experts—for example, the bomb squad if you have a military collection—should go on your list with important contacts.

The "feeling" for your collection might also touch on legal or ethical aspects. If you find objects that look like they could be Native American, they might fall under the *Native American Graves Protection and Repatriation Act (NAGPRA)*[2]. You might not be immediately aware if this is the case or not, so put these items aside as you work through the collection. You can't be sure if these objects have a ritual significance and special restrictions so, if possible, store them in the most respectful way at a place where they won't be touched or handled until someone who knows about them can take a look. Once you determine whether or not the questioned objects do belong to a Native American tribe, then you will need to research the proper procedures and who to contact to assist in those procedures.

If there are taxidermy specimens, other forms of preserved natural objects, or objects made out of animal skin or feathers, take into account that they might fall under the Convention on International Trade in Endangered Species of Wild Fauna and Flora (CITES).[3] Whether or not you have objects that are CITES regulated, you should still make yourself familiar with the regulations and research for an expert in your area/region should you need to contact someone for assistance.

Issues That Have To Be Resolved

This will be a list of all the issues you spotted and that need to be resolved in order to document, store and preserve the collection for future generations. It will be a long list and most certainly you will separate it into two lists later: a list of things you can do yourself and a list of things that need to be done by others.

When you have your first long list go through it and give the issues a priority. You can go into detail later, for a start just use numbers 1–3:

Priority 1: has to be resolved before anyone can start working with the collection.
Priority 2: can be done while working with the collection but should be done as soon as possible.
Priority 3: important but can wait a little longer.

Resist the urge to file everything in category 1. This category is reserved for the really, really important issues. When the roof is in such bad shape that there is a risk it will crash and bury the collection, that's definitely a priority 1. If there is a hole in the roof that becomes bigger but no water reaches the room with the collection you will have a priority 2, even if it's certainly not good to have a hole in the roof. If there is a small but stable hole in the roof that lets a few drops of water through only when there are heavy rainfalls and wind from the northeast it might even be just a priority 3.

As in emergency planning, when assigning a priority to a task you have to weigh the likeliness of something happening against the impact it will have on the collection you care for. Priorities can vary widely, such as geographical implications, or the delicacy of the collection's items, and do not forget extrinsic factors like deadlines for grants or board decisions all play a role in this.

When you've finished the list prioritizing tasks, you split it into two lists: The first one will include all the tasks you can do by yourself. This will be the list that defines your next concrete tasks, ordered by priority. Your second list will mention all the tasks for which you need someone else to help. It might make it easier to have this list in a spreadsheet with four columns: task, priority, what has to be done by someone else and who this someone is, and a preferred date of completion. In the beginning, the first list will be rather

Figure 3.1. Making sure those wires dangling from the empty light fix-ture are not energised is definitely a priority 1, before anyone is allowed to work in this room. Courtesy of the Museum of Danish America, Elk Horn, Iowa.

small and the second very long. Without proper working conditions you will not be able to do much. This will change throughout the progress. Tables 3.1 and 3.2 are examples of the two lists so you get the picture.

As said in chapter 1, it's best to split tasks into small steps. Tasks with top priority might take some time to be completed but don't need your close

Table 3.1.   Tasks with priority and estimated date of completion

Task	Priority	Date of completion
Complete list with needed tools and materials—to have it approved by the board	1	March 2 (board meeting is March 3)
Research all relevant information for applying for IMLS grant	2	July 1 (so there is enough time to write actual application that has December 1 as deadline)
Clear working space in collections area	2	as soon as bomb squad has declared area safe (approx. some days after January 17)
Sort the collection to begin cataloging (see chapter 5, "Diving into the Collection" for details)	3	June 1

Table 3.2. Tasks with priority and responsibility

Task	Priority	Who does it?	Date of completion
Examine bomb shells and ammunition in collections area	1	bomb squad	January 17
Fix hole in roof	2	roofer	after board has accepted roofer's offer (approx. March)
Approve list of needed tools and materials	2	board	March 3 (board meeting)
Fix leaky window in collections area	3	Paul, me	after bomb squad has declared collections area safe (approx. some days after January 17)

attention all the time. In the meantime you can work on smaller tasks with lower priority. While waiting for the approval to buy shelving units and packing materials, you can easily sort parts of the collection and clean out the aisles.

One common mistake is to be focused so much on the things with top priority that one forgets to look to see if the effort put into this is worth it. For example, if some official is in charge of deciding if the roof is repaired or not, it certainly is recommended to keep track of the progress, and send a reminder every now and then, but it doesn't help to phone this person frequently. There is a Chinese saying that goes, "The grass doesn't grow faster if you pull it." Some things need their time and in the meantime there is time for other things.

Things You Will Need

This list will contain a whole range of things: tools, packaging materials, tables, a chair, a camera. Put down everything you noticed you will need, then think of what else could be missing. Put them all down, even if you think that some things are really expensive and you won't get them fast, if you get them at all. You never know, sometimes an opportunity arises and there are a few dollars left in someone's budget—and exclusively for office furniture or camera equipment. Then it's good to come up with a suggestion of what to buy right on the spot.

Having said that, it's good to do research on what those materials cost and to note prices, manufacturers, and retailers. This will give you an idea of the amount of money the equipment and materials you need will cost. In some cases it might make sense to think about alternatives right from the start. For example, What does a really good camera with equipment cost (think also about lights and necessary setups for really good pictures)? And what are acceptable alternatives that might give you pictures that are good enough for documentation, although maybe not good enough for publication?

When you have completed this list, define priorities as you already have with the issues that have to be resolved:

Priority 1: what is needed to work with the collection immediately;
Priority 2: what can be bought while working with the collection, but should be bought soon; and
Priority 3: what can wait a little longer but is needed for proper care in the long run.

For example, you won't be able to do anything without a desk, some tables, a computer, and some working material like gloves and pens. These are Priority 1 items, things you will need to survive the first few weeks. In most

Figure 3.2.   The trunks that you saw in figure 3.1 in their new compact shelving. Getting there needs time and endurance, but it can be done. Courtesy of the Museum of Danish America, Elk Horn, Iowa.

cases a vacuum cleaner with a HEPA filter is also a Priority 1 item; working in a dusty environment will make it impossible to care for the collection properly. Packing materials and storage furniture are crucial, but as you start off with sorting and researching they might get a Priority 2 assignment. You need to take photographs right from the start and certainly need a camera for documentation, so you might argue that a camera is a Priority 1 item. But if you have a camera that takes pictures, just not good pictures, better camera equipment might be a Priority 3 to you.

A good question is whether you should communicate those priorities to upper management. It depends on so many factors that there is no clear answer to this question. Some decision makers prefer to see the whole list, work through it point by point, and then give you the permission to buy whatever you think is right as long as you don't spend more than a certain amount. Others want to know what you will need immediately and what you will need in the long run so they can think about where and how to source those things. Still others want to go into every detail and make many, small, detailed decisions. Find out what kinds of decision makers you are dealing with and structure your "official" list accordingly. Of course, if you are fully in charge of sourcing the materials yourself, including finding the money, sharing priorities isn't a concern. Read chapter 9, "We Had Nothing," for ideas.

THE LEGAL STATUS

Working with a collection means investing a lot of time and effort. You might assume that the collection belongs to the institution you are working for, but this isn't necessarily the case. Collections sometimes just "pile up" over a number of years and nobody thought of having the legal status secured in terms of documents. You should make sure that all the objects you are dealing with actually belong to your institution before you start to invest time and money into them. To make yourself aware of the issues involved with securing the legal status, read *A Legal Primer on Managing Museum Collections*,[4] especially chapter 4 about the acquisition of objects. If parts of your collection are already accessioned and others aren't, and you are not completely sure about the status of still others, reading *Collection Conundrums*[5] can help you to decide what to do.

If the collection comes from one single donor, finding out about the legal status should be easy: There should be a deed of gift or a document that states the will of the collector to give his or her collection to the museum or whatever institution you work for. If such a document doesn't exist, try to get one. If you are lucky, you will find correspondence, a draft of a deed of gift, or other documents that show the intention of the donor. If you find nothing like this, things get complicated. You might need the help of a lawyer, especially if the donor has passed away since the donation.

If the collection was built up over time things can become a bit tricky. As a general approach, try to find all the documents related to the collection. This can become nerve-wracking if all the objects were given to the museum by community members over time to "build a museum" and no one cared about paperwork. Prepare for a lot of legwork here. In this case it's something that can't be done before you actually start working with the collection. It will be an ongoing task while cataloging the collection. However, you should always try to determine if the object belongs to your institution or not before you invest time in cataloging, packing, and storing. When in doubt it might be wiser to put an object aside until the legal status is secured.

There is a strange thing with collections: as long as objects are away from the public eye, in storage, and no one does anything with them, they are easily forgotten. But as soon as they are cleaned, repaired, and presented in an exhibition, their status changes in the eyes of many people. Most collections managers have a story that goes more or less like this: A certain object—let's make it a hand-colored Frisbee®—was in storage for about twenty years. It is presented in the new exhibition on youth culture in the last century. A few days after the opening someone calls, claiming that the Frisbee belonged to his family, was hand-colored by his own father, and therefore has a high nostalgic value. In a lucky outcome, they just want you to add this story to your documentation, but more likely they want the object back, a donation plaque, or a tax deduction.

To avoid complications in the future, secure the legal status at the earliest point possible, because you never know when you will need to prove it and for what reasons. Never delay or neglect it. There is a mantra for this, which I have borrowed from a colleague I hold in high esteem, Tracey Berg-Fulton: "Be kind to your future self."[6]

THE COLLECTIONS POLICY

A collections policy is the basis both for working with the collection and for the future development of the collection. It elaborates on the mission statement of what your institution collects, how it does it, and why.[7] A collections policy helps to determine if you should accession an object or not. When working with an unmanaged collection, a collections policy serves as your compass. There will be numerous objects which you are in doubt about whether you should keep and accession them; your collection policy will help you both with making the decision and with explaining the reasons for your decision to others. If there is no collections policy, establishing one will be a top priority on your to-do list.

Especially if you are the "hands on" kind of person who likes to get stuff done, you might wonder if a collections policy is really necessary and if it would not be better to first look at what objects your collection consists of and then write the policy. This might sound logical, but it means giving away what is perhaps the only really big advantage of an unmanaged collection. Writing collection policies for already existing and cataloged collections almost always means to compromise. For example, the collection of 473 soldering irons does not fit into your mission and your scope of collections, but it is already accessioned and published, so instead of deaccessioning them, you have to find a way to define in your collections policy how they fit into your scope.

With an unmanaged collection you have the chance to define what fits into the collection before you know in detail what objects you have. This makes your decisions more rational and helps with the actual work on the collection. For example, if you suspect that your institution is unable to care for textiles properly and you know that there is a museum that specializes in historical dresses of your region, it is logical to define that you won't collect dresses and offer whatever dress you find to the mentioned other museum. It is much easier to define policies at this early stage than once you have already fallen in love with the beautiful wedding dress or the Civil War uniform you find while working in the collection.

For a start, read *The AAM Guide to Collections Planning*, especially the chapters "Building the Intellectual Framework" and "Writing the Collections Plan."[8] When you actually write the plan, *Things Great and Small* by John E. Simmons is a very detailed and helpful resource. [9] For the legal aspects, read chapter 3 on collections management policies in the already mentioned *Legal Primer*.[10]

Writing a collections policy takes time and you might not be the person responsible for the final version or for putting it into effect. It is an illusion to have a perfectly crafted collections policy before laying hands on the collection. But what you should have before you start your actual work is a clearly defined scope of collections, something that tells you what you should accession and which objects have to find another place. While your completed collections policy might be a multipage document, for a start some simple sentences can be just as helpful. "We collect objects that were common in the households of our town between 1850 and 1950," is a clear statement that sets a time frame and a range of objects. Sure, in detail there will be numerous objects to argue about. Is a car an item of a household? One citizen lived in South Africa between 1895 and 1905, so is the lion skin he used as a carpet a "common" household item? Is a chest that was built by an ancestor around 1500 but was used by a citizen until 1989 part of the scope? You will have to think, define, and maybe adjust while working, but instead of working blindly, you will already have a definition to use.

If you are still not convinced that a collections policy is a necessary first step, there is one more real life experience that speaks in its favor: As soon as the word spreads that someone is caring for the collection, it is very likely that people will be willing to help you and the museum. Some people want to help you by donating more objects. While this is a noble thought, it means that you have to deal not only with the existing unmanaged collection, but also with object offers. While it is generally recommended to explain that you won't start to collect actively as long as the existing collection is not documented, you should be already able to tell your community in what direction you will collect.

THE COLLECTION MANAGEMENT SYSTEM

Whether you like it or not, you will probably need a collection management system (CMS) in the long run. There are several on the market and you might even find it tempting to build one yourself or just work with a spreadsheet software. The decision about which system to use is a crucial one and it is highly recommended that one researches this topic thoroughly before making a decision.[11] Make sure to check with a lot of colleagues who work in institutions comparable to your own. A colleague from a large institution with a lot of loans may praise a CMS that has a lot of options to include contracts, condition reports, and insurance documents, but it might be too complex and expensive for what you need in a small museum. A colleague from a natural history museum might prefer a CMS with many features and fields that are irrelevant for a historical collection, and vice versa. Another colleague might find a certain CMS extremely easy to use, but only because he started his career as a software engineer. If possible, try to see as many collection management systems in everyday use as you can. Preferably let colleagues show it to you, not the software manufacturer. Ask these colleagues what they like about the system, what they don't like, what common issues are, and why they chose this particular software over another. This will tell you more than any research you will be able to conduct.

Be careful considering do-it-yourself (DIY) systems; as you continue documenting your collection you create more and more data and therefore more complex software issues. You might find yourself being more of a software engineer than a collections manager. Some DIY solutions in small museums become unusable when its creator retires, a software update eliminates a certain feature, or the software itself isn't supported by a new operating system.

When choosing a system, consider who will have to work with it in the long run. Especially if you are quite computer savvy yourself you might not be the best to decide if a system is user-friendly. Be aware that you will probably not be the one who makes the database entries in the future and that the quality of object data is dependent upon how easy or hard it is to enter data correctly. To make the most educated decision, let some people who are typical future users type in a few sample object records and let them tell you what they like about the system and where there are obstacles.

When choosing, anticipate how your institution will probably develop in the future. If collections care and database entries will be mainly in the hands of volunteers with little computer knowledge, you will probably have to decide on an easier-to-use and less complex system than if you are responsible for an university collection that will always have a decent number of student computer geeks around who are able to hack the code of the database and rewrite it if necessary. The accessibility of your data and the longevity of the chosen system will highly depend on how good you are in deciding what will work in your setting.

For a start it might be best to work with spreadsheet software, but keep in mind that a collection management system might be needed in the future. Be sure to structure your data in a way that it can be imported into a common database system. The spreadsheet software and the collection management system should be part of your list of needed materials.

THE EVENING ROUTINE

Having read so far you will have realized that there is a lot of decision making in the process. Sure, some of these decisions are not up to you in the final stage, but there are many, many small decisions that are. Most of your decisions might look totally logical and intuitive to you at the very moment you make them. But only a few weeks or months later you will wonder why you have done certain things that way. That's why it's a good idea to start a diary as soon as you start working with the collection. It should be like a navigation book of your collections work. Take down what you decided and why in a short, concise way. Also take notes on unusual occurrences or observations. You sometimes have the impression that there was something odd, but can't remember when you first realized it. This might sound rather theoretically, so table 3.3 shows three sample entries.

Table 3.3. Example of diary

April 13, 2015	Signed contract with Smith & Sons for all heating, roof, and water maintenance. Cheaper than the three separate contracts we had with three separate firms and Mr. Smith was recommended by Springfield's Soldering Iron Museum's director, who said they are very reliable and very quick in response to emergencies.
May 12, 2015	8:05 Found window in collection room slightly open. Paul says he's nearly sure it wasn't when he worked inside yesterday afternoon. No signs of physical damage or attempts to open it with brute force. Must observe.
May 20, 2015	Numbered shelves. Rows are A–F, columns are 1–5, so we can number the shelves when we continue to clear the space toward the windows. Estimate that we will end up with A 1–10, B 1–10, and C 1–10, and D 1–15, E 1 15, and F 1 15 once we have enough money for complete shelving.

You can use a paper calendar, a paper notebook, or a computer program, but make sure that the diary is easy to find. It might be that you can't continue working with the collection immediately or even that you have to cease working with it at all. By having the diary in an accessible place, you make sure that whenever some other colleagues or you have the chance to resume the work, it is easy to understand why something was done and where it makes sense to continue working.

The diary can be the first or the last step in your regular evening routine. During the day you will take some notes by hand and make some changes in the computer. Your evening routine should make sure that you are on the same page on both systems. Add appointments you made during the day to your calendar software, update contact information you got via e-mail with your paper address book, make sure the documents in your file folders or binders are up-to-date. If you use a digital camera, save to your computer pictures you took during the day. Make sure you back up your computer files regularly, which also includes printing important information to have it in paper form in case of a computer breakdown.

The evening routine should always end your day, no matter how stressful it was. Because it has become a habit, implementing this routine early in the process will help you to keep it up even in chaotic times. It also sets a clear end to your working day and helps you to relax in the evening.

THE FIRST LOGICAL EXIT

After a lot of hard work you have completed all necessary tasks for the first logical exit. As said in the preface, logical exits are safe places to reach.

With a logical exit reached, you can take a break and resume the work later without risking that you have to start all over again. At this first logical exit you should have

- a compilation of all basic information concerning the collection's environment, both in electronic and paper form.
- all relevant information at the places you will most likely need them—that is, the heating manual and telephone number of the service technician in the heating room, for example.
- a list of books, loads of PDFs and other documents, and probably a whole file folder with printed-out information concerning different collections items and materials.
- two lists of issues to tackle—one with tasks you can do on your own and one with tasks with which you will need help in the forms of money, material, and/or staff—and both lists should be ordered by priority.
- a list of materials you will need to start working.
- a collection of legal documents concerning the collection's items, although this might be a work in progress.
- a collections policy, although this might be only a draft.
- a diary of decisions and occurrences.

Congratulations on the accomplishment! You can now either proceed with the next step, hand the lists over to those who are responsible for deciding how to go on, or take a break from working with the collection and come back to it later. The latter might especially apply for directors of small museums who are juggling their different responsibilities. With your information well structured you can go back to work on the collection during the next off-season or when time allows.

NOTES

1. John Campbell, "Fire Grenades," *North Carolina Connecting to Collections Blog*, https://collectionsconversations.wordpress.com/2014/09/09/fire-grenades/

2. *Native American Graves Protection and Repatriation Act*, Pub. L. No. 101-601, 25 U.S.C. 3001-3013, http://www.gpo.gov/fdsys/pkg/STATUTE-104/pdf/STAT-UTE-104-Pg3048.pdf.

3. Convention on International Trade in Endangered Species of Wild Fauna and Flora (CITES), signed in Washington, DC, May 3, 1973, https://www.cites.org/.

4. Marie C. Malaro and Ildiko P. DeAngelis, *A Legal Primer on Managing Museum Collections* (Washington, DC: Smithsonian Books, 2012).

5. Rebecca A. Buck and Jean A. Gilmore, eds., *Collection Conundrums: Solving Collections Management Mysteries* (Washington, DC: AAM Press, 2007).

6. Used in the presentation, "We Were Promised Jetpacks: What Does the Future Hold for Registrars?" on June 10 at the European Registrars Conference 2013 in Helsinki.

7. Actually, you might need three documents: a collections policy (what your institution collects and why), a collections plan (how your institution will collect now and in the future) and a collections management policy (how you work with the collection and how you care for it). However, as the collections policy is the basis of the other two documents and the one you need most urgently for starting to work with the collection, I suggest starting with the collections policy to keep it simple. Then as there's time and you've begun to build your procedures and defined how to move forward, the other two documents can be written.

8. James B. Gardener and Elizabeth E. Merrit, *The AAM Guide to Collections Planning* (Washington, DC: AAM Press, 2004).

9. John E. Simmons, *Things Great and Small: Collections Management Policies* (Washington, DC: AAM Press, 2006).

10. Marie C. Malaro and Ildiko P. DeAngelis, *A Legal Primer on Managing Museum Collections* (Washington, DC: Smithsonian Books, 2012).

11. You can compare some of the most widely used collections management software on the website of the Collections Trust, http://www.collectionstrust.org.uk/choose-a-cms, but be aware that you are only able to compare the technical and economical aspects, while you have to check usability for yourself.

Chapter Four

Getting Organized

Until this point you have gathered and structured information, set your priorities and presumably brought your upper management to start some processes in decision making and money granting. You have your priority list, so it's very obvious what the burning issues with the collection are and what needs to be done first. But before you can actually start working with the collection you need to do a few more things:

- You need to develop a location system so you can track objects and issues.
- You need to organize the space you will be working in.
- You have to fix the most pressing issues, at least temporarily, so the place is safe for your objects and everybody who is working with the collection.

This is a key step—the transition from an unmanaged place with a lot of old stuff in it to a place where a responsible collections manager has taken the lead. Yes, this collections manager is you. If you manage to follow it through to the next logical exit, this change will be obvious, even to outsiders.

WHERE WAS THAT THING AGAIN?

In order to manage a collection you need to have an effective system to retrieve your objects. You can't delay this until you have appropriate storage furniture. When working with the collection, you have to define where things are right from the start.

If you work in a larger institution like a farming museum with several houses and sheds, this will be slightly different from a museum where the whole collection is stored in a single room. However, the general approach is always the same: start with numbering the larger units like rooms and break it down step by step until you reach the smallest logical unit, which can be a shelving unit, shelf, or archival box.

In an institution with various buildings, start with numbering the buildings, then number the rooms. Keep in mind that having descriptive names can be helpful in human conversation, but can be tricky when you change the purpose of the rooms. If you have multiple buildings it is advisable to use the same pattern of numbering the rooms in every building. If you started numbering the rooms in "Building 1" with the first room on the first floor on

---

A REAL-WORLD EXAMPLE

It is tempting to name rooms after the collections that are stored in them. This might work but can become problematic if there is a reorganization in storage, so additional numbers are always preferable. But there is one approach that is even more problematic. I worked for an institution that named the collection rooms after the curator responsible for that part of the collection. So instead of a "textile room" and a "toy room" they had a "Miller room" and a "Smith room" (names changed to protect the innocent). Needless to say, curators retired and new ones came. As there was no consistent location code, typically rooms kept the name of the former curator except for some cases where the new curator aggressively insisted on a new name for the room. This meant that every new employee had to learn the staff history to find things. And of course, because the naming was inconsistent, some rooms had up to four different names that were used in everyday conversation— which lead to hilarious dialogues and misunderstandings. Of course, as old habits die hard, the everyday use of the terms stayed in place even after the rooms were numbered consistently, so new employees still had to learn the old terms to work with more seasoned staff members.

A: "It's in Smith's room."

B: "Smith's room? Is it room 3?"

A: "What's room 3? Is it where Linda works?"

B: "No, that's room 5."

A: "Smith's room is the small one near the stair case, you know, the one where the spinning wheels and the woodworking tools are stored."

B: "Ah, I see, so it's room 8. Thanks."

the left hand side being "Room 1" and numbered the rooms from there on working clockwise, the same should be done in "Building 2" up to "Building X" to avoid confusion.

So, you found the room, but how can you find things inside the room? Like descriptive names of rooms, directions tend to be vague and lead to misunderstandings. "There's a water leak at the far right end of the room," "the second window facing south" or "below the last shelf on the left wall" might seem unmistakably clear to you but not to the one you are talking to. The number of people who confuse left and right is considerably high (the author included) and only few people know the cardinal direction of a building they are not completely familiar with. So, you need a better system.

A good approach is to lay an imaginary grid over the whole storage room, the way road maps are done. Take a look at Graph 4.1 to see an example. Think of the room as a giant chessboard. It is not necessary that every single grid square is really square. It's more important that the squares are easy to spot. Supports like steel beams are "natural" separators of grids; so are windows and doors. Even electric cables or pipelines can serve as markers.

Like a chessboard, every square is defined by a number and a letter. I found it helpful to stay in the logic of the chessboard, so my grid is always oriented in the way that the letters run from left to right of a room, while numbers start at the entrance door and run toward the opposite wall. How large the squares should be is defined by the nature of the room and the collection. At the storage of the TECHNOSEUM, the grids are about 16' x 16', which is great for big machinery and midsize collection items like TV sets. Combined with numbered, heavy-duty racks, shelving units, or boxes, the chessboard method is a very powerful tool for all sizes of collections items, down to the size of a gramophone needle. In smaller rooms you will need smaller squares, in very small rooms the grid structure might not be helpful at all and you directly go to numbering shelving units.

The big advantage of the chessboard method is that you can define where things are even if the collection is in an unordered, piled up state. It helps defining and remembering where you spotted objects that contain hazardous materials, where you put the mouse traps, or where the water pipe is dripping. Make sure to draw a plan of the grid, put it in your files, and hand it out to everyone who works with the collection so they are able to find things and report incidents. It pays to have one plan hung in the collections room it depicts.

If you have storage furniture already it is a good idea to number it right from the start, too. Numbering storage furniture in a concise way that allows enough flexibility for growth and change is a complex task. It is discussed thoroughly along with other important storage organization methods in chapter 8, "Storage Wants and Storage Needs."

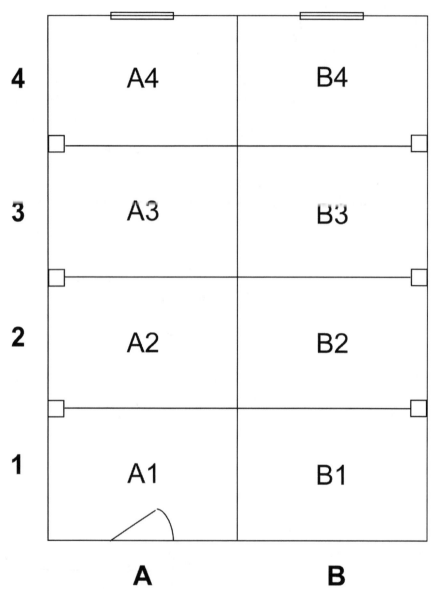

Graph 4.1.   Example grid laid over a small room

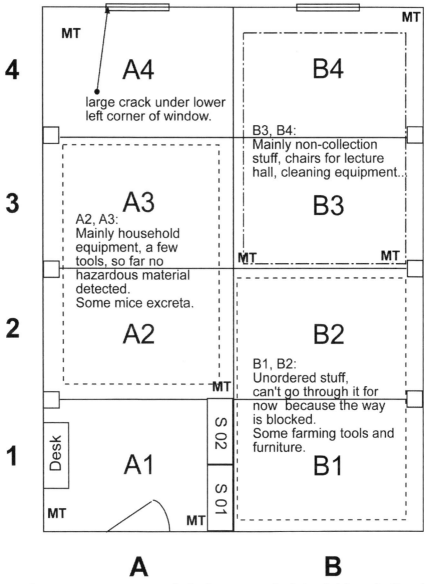

4

MT

A4

large crack under lower
left corner of window.

B4

MT

3

A3

A2, A3:
Mainly household
equipment, a few
tools, so far no
hazardous material
detected.
Some mice excreta.

B3, B4:
Mainly non-collection
stuff, chairs for lecture
hall, cleaning equipment...

B3

MT   MT

2

A2

B2

MT

B1, B2:
Unordered stuff,
can't go through it for
now because the way
is blocked.
Some farming tools and
furniture.

1

Desk

A1

S 02

S 01

B1

MT   MT

A

B

Graph 4.2.   How your room may look when you noted existing shelving units (S) and
where you put the mouse traps (MT)

THE GRANDMOTHER'S FIXES

I like to refer to the next set of steps as "Grandmother's Fixes" because grandmothers are great at fixing problems, may it be a broken vase, finger, or heart. Especially since they know when it's time to roll up the sleeves and start working and when it's time to stop and think over the next steps. They have gained a lot of experience in carrying a family through rough times of scarce resources. The Grandmother's Fixes are about improving things right then and there with your own hands and with stuff that is available and costs little to no money. Of course, you shouldn't try to fix a broken vase with superglue like your real grandmother would. The grandmother I want you to have in mind is an ideal grandmother, an easy-to-imagine superheroine with the superpowers of common sense and creativity. A very old, very wise, and very caring super-heroine who helps you to determine what to do next. "Grandmother" with a capital "G" on her apron; that's her.

There is a hidden danger in this approach: It might create the delusion that all issues can be fixed with little to no money, and so, the collection doesn't need money to be managed. But this isn't true. Preserving a collection is an investment. To reach a managed collection someday you will need to buy materials, storage furniture, and pay for professional repairs and professional help. You might even need a new storage area. Grandmother's Fixes are just about doing something about the worst issues so you can start working before these resources come in—not a substitute for them. It's important to point out this fact to upper management or they might get the idea that Grandmother's Fixes are enough for safeguarding the collection.

So, look at the collection through the eyes of Grandmother and ask yourself what you can do immediately with the limited resources you have now.

Is It Art or Is It Trash?

In a well-managed collection you will find materials stored separately from the objects, and the work places will not be in the same room as the collection. Chances are the situation you encountered on your first day didn't even look a bit like that. You don't have to reach ideal storage conditions right from the start, but you have to get this place organized so you and other people can work in it safely and effectively. The good news is that this can be done right away, without additional resources.

First, try to get rid of everything that is obviously trash. Sometimes this can be tricky to define. Be very careful with things that lie in close proximity to objects that are undoubtedly collections items, for there might be a connection. When in doubt, don't throw it away. But in every unmanaged collection

I ever saw, the room was used as temporary storage for things that weren't needed anymore and that should have been thrown away much earlier.

If you come across problematic substances like batteries, chemicals, or burned out neon lights, you may encounter the problem of having to dispose of them professionally, which will probably cost money. In this case find a place where you can store them safely and away from the collection. Make sure you label them properly so everybody can see why this material was moved here, when, and by whom. For example, those labels could read "Dispose of," "Recycle" or "Hazardous" (preferably with a notation of what it contains), followed by a date and the initials of the colleague who put it there.[1] Working with packing tape in different colors can make it easier to spot the different categories of trash.

Disposing of these substances and materials should be regarded as high priority, because there is an inherent danger for them to be near the collection and they take up space without being of any use. You might try to reach an agreement with your local waste management company to dispose of them for free as a donation to your institution.

Another material group that should be stored separately are things you need for working with the collection or that are needed in the institution but that aren't collections items. These can be cleaning supplies, tools, IT equipment, exhibit cases, chairs for events, and so forth, the possibilities are endless. Your aim should be to get them out of the storage room and keep them out. There's a variation on Murphy's Law that is known as "Boston's Irreversible Law of Clutter," and it says, "In any household, junk accumulates to fill the space available for its storage."[2] This is also true for museum storage. The moment you defined a space where this non-collection material should be stored—which can also be a separate part of the room the collection is in, if there is no other room available—it will be a constant battle to keep it there, but a battle worth fighting.

How Bad Is That Crack, Really?

When you inspected the building your collection is stored in, you should have made a list of issues. Look at those you have marked as top priorities and determine if you can fix some of them with what you've got at the moment. Grandmother's Fixes on building issues are often about doing something very obvious: putting buckets under a leaking roof, closing a broken window with some old wooden boards, or pulling objects away from a wet wall. (But be careful to document the move in pictures; you might destroy connections between objects.) It's surprising how often simple fixes aren't done. Sometimes because they are overlooked; sometimes because everybody determined it's not in his or her job description; sometimes because one waits for a professional to fix it—who, if there is no money to pay him/her, may not come for the next couple of years.

As every collection and every building is different, it is impossible to list all possible issues and all possible fixes. Grandmother's Fixes are not things you can recommend as general approaches on how to fix issues, because they depend on your special situation and the things you have available. When you use Grandmother's Fixes, you use your own imagination, your creativity, and your knowledge about your objects to find a fix for a burning collections issue. Just as an example to make the concept clear, I'll take the common hole—a connection between the outside and the inside of a building that provides access for all kind of pests. Obviously, this entrance should be closed to the best of your ability immediately. A hole in the wall might be fixed with old newspaper crammed into it, a gap between door and floor might be closed with a sandbag, an odd-shaped crack in the wall might be filled with construction foam.

Sure, you won't find any recommendations for those repairs in books about collection care—and for a good reason. In a well-managed collection you should be very careful about what materials you use and should strive for the safest, inert materials you can find. However, at the moment when you are

---

A REAL-WORLD EXAMPLE

Sometimes "Grandmother's Fixes" are unbelievably simple. One of the former off-site storages of the Landesmuseum für Technik und Arbeit[1] in Mannheim was a large industrial hall and its roof consisted of more than 50 percent glass windows. That's why this hall was incredibly bright but also incredibly unsuitable for the storage of objects. The fix, or at least major improvement, was incredibly simple: our painter painted the windows white. This reduced the light level significantly, cost only a few buckets of paint, and was done in just a few days.

Notes

1. The Landesmuseum für Technik und Arbeit was rebranded into TECH-NOSEUM—Landesmuseum für Technik und Arbeit in 2009. I will use the former name for events that happened before 2009 and the latter whenever I refer to more recent events and everything that refers to my institution in general.

working in the less-than-ideal world of an unmanaged collection, the actual damage done by mice, bats, or birds coming in through the holes is a much bigger problem than potential outgassing or deterioration of the materials you have at hand to apply those fixes. You should make sure however that whatever you do is reversible and your fixes can be replaced by more professional repairs later.

Grandmother's Fixes are only good if you are fully aware of what you are doing. A good example is mold: Your real grandmother might have had a whole range of chemicals to deal with mold, but mold is definitely a case for a specialist. You shouldn't try to fix this issue with any common household remedies. Your issue with mold is twofold: You have to find the cause and cure the symptoms. Spotting the cause will most likely be easier than finding a cure. The wet cellar with insufficient ventilation is pretty obvious, but space, material, and time to take any single object out, treat it sufficiently, and store it in a better place is yet to be sourced. Grandmother will most certainly recommend that you talk to someone who knows about mold, educate yourself, and develop a plan on how to deal with the situation before you actually go in there. You might want to send a sample to a specialist to analyze what kind of mold you are dealing with so you know what safety precautions you have to take. Oh, and, "Kid, don't forget your mask!"

Create A Place To Work

In nearly every unmanaged collection, area space is scarce. Unfortunately, to work with the collection you need even more space. So, the next thing to do is locate a place where you can create space. You need a place to set up your working table, a place where you can sit and write down things. It is ideal if there is an outlet so you can work on a computer or laptop, if you are lucky enough to have electricity in your building.

Furthermore, you need space to examine and sort things. Even in a collection that consists of mainly big objects like agricultural machines, cars, or industrial machinery you will need at least one table to sort smaller things like spare parts or instruction manuals. In a collection with smaller parts, a set of tables is recommended. Additionally, you need to create space for another table that is reserved for taking pictures of objects. If the building doesn't have tables, they should be relatively easy to get. Ask around, many people have unused tables in their cellars—not to forget the tool my dear colleague Darlene Bialowski calls the "best assistant of the non-human variety": the sawhorse.[3] With a pair of sawhorses and an old door or any kind of wooden board you can create a very portable flat surface in a convenient size.

Figure 4.1. Start working—but where? You first need to create some space. Courtesy of the Museum of Danish America, Elk Horn, Iowa.

How do you clear space in a situation where you can't just start in one corner because, literally, there is no corner? Well, you need Grandmother's creativity, the same creativity that made children's trousers out of worn-out blankets. You need to spot the possibilities you have and use them in the best possible way.

In the theory of storage planning and preservation, it is prohibited to pile objects, for very good reasons like access and the risk of damage in long-term storage or when taking objects out. In the reality of the unmanaged collection, you have to create a way to work with the collection, otherwise you risk more damage and loss than books about preventive conservation have in mind. But that's also why chapter 3 discussed the importance of getting a "feeling" for your objects. A clean cardboard box can be stored on a dresser without doing any damage to the dresser, but you shouldn't put a greasy oil can on that same dresser. A bed frame will be fine leaning against a wall while an oil painting can suffer. Cupboards have an interior and cars have luggage trunks where something can be stored temporarily (don't forget to take notes and pictures of what you put where). Yes, this has little to do with preferable museum storage, but as things are now, you are far from that anyway, so let's use Grandmother's common sense.

Once you have taken the first steps toward creating space, it will become easier. In many unmanaged collections you have to gnaw your path into the collection, creating aisles and space for setting up shelving units step by step.

Figure 4.2. The same room as depicted in Figure 4.1, after reorganization. A great place to work in. Courtesy of the Museum of Danish America, Elk Horn, Iowa.

Organize the Work

Every real grandmother has some common proverbs and key sentences she will repeat over and over again, so often that they become famous family slogans, passed through the generations. The key phrase of Grandmother is "A place for everything and everything in its place." Right from the start you should define a place where the materials and tools are stored, from where they can be taken out of and returned to. You can define this even before you have actually bought any tools or materials.

It is as important to define the place where trash is stored until it is finally disposed of—preferably not in the same room as the collection. For some trash like metal, you might even get some money from a recycler, so sort the trash if possible. Just as important as a separate place for the trash is the need to have a trash bag—or even a few—at the place where the collection is stored so you can throw something away immediately without interrupting your work flow. Make sure that those bags are taken out every evening, especially if compostable or hazardous stuff was thrown away.

Another important place is the space where one is allowed to eat. This can't be in the collection's room; that goes without saying. Define this place, which wherever possible should be a separate room. There also has to be a facility to wash your hands before you eat, either in the same room or in a separate room, and a place where you can safely store the protective clothing. This applies even if you are the only staff member and belong to the rare species of museum professionals that lives on looking at artifacts and drinking a glass of water a day. There will be a time when you will have a volunteer, intern, or visiting expert in the collection. Stating "this is the place where we eat and drink" in a matter-of-fact way right in the beginning is much easier than explaining why eating in the collection is not allowed once the peanut butter and jelly sandwich is unwrapped.

CONTROLLED ACCESS

You want to control access to the place your collection is stored for a variety of reasons. The earlier you can enforce this, the better. Now that you've organized the space and want it to stay that way, it's high time to organize access. At this very moment in the process of organizing the collection, you have one big advantage: The collection still looks like a mess. No director, board member or mayor would be willing to show it proudly to donors, politicians, or family members. When this collection is clean, well ordered, and in a "best practice" state, this will be a whole different story, and as you are working toward this direction, time for restricting access unhindered is running out.

Your first step will be to find out who holds keys to the collection area. In older institutions, this will be impossible and you will have to find money to replace the locks, soon. In the unlikely event that you can track all keys, your next step is to define who really needs them. You will encounter more people who think they need them than who really do need them and should have them. In smaller institutions, three keys should be sufficient: one for the one responsible for the collection, one for his or her assistant or other representative who is caring for the collection when the responsible staff is on holiday or ill, and one that is stored at a safe place in case of emergency.

There are a variety of occasions that might make it necessary to have more keys. But these reasons should be examined very carefully. Fewer keys mean, almost without exception, more security. It even helps reasoning with upper management: it's easier to explain that only the collections manager and his or her assistant hold a key and even the director is dependent on them to get access to storage than to explain why the janitor and one curator hold a key while a board member has only access accompanied by the collections manager.

One should be aware that access to a storage area holds a highly emotional component. Keys are symbols of power in our Western hemisphere and you should be aware that taking the key from someone is a humiliating gesture, even if everybody involved in this process agrees that it makes sense to control the access. It might be preferable simply for this reason to replace the lock and have only the necessary number of keys for the new one.

The rules of access to the collection should be part of your collections policy. Along with the definition of who holds keys to the collection and why—defined by position or job title in the institution, not actual persons—the procedure of how to get access to the collection needs to be described. The keys should be numbered and each key holder should sign for the receipt of the key in an attachment to the policy. Make sure to include language that the key holder agrees with this statement that the keys must not be duplicated or lent to unauthorized personnel.

Who accesses the collection and why should be documented in a suitable manner, noting name, date, and reason. For your assisting staff (like interns and volunteers) and you, documentation of your working hours might be sufficient. For all others there should be a logbook or some other kind of tracking method.

Enforcing restricted access is a nerve-wracking process that needs time, patience, and mental balance. It will probably be a procedure you are still defending when your collection has been in a well-ordered state for the longest time. Consistency is key. If you allow access for a volunteer without being accompanied by you or your assistant one time, you'll have a very hard time explaining why your director can't hold a key. Enforce the access policy with the three *p*s: persistence, patience, and politeness. Explain why it's important over and over again, don't get angry if you have to explain it for the 4,657th time to the same person, and don't create precedents by allowing exemptions from the access rules written down in the collections policy.

A GUIDED TOUR OF PROFESSIONAL CARE

You will remember that I've said at the beginning of this chapter that what is done in this step is a key step in the process, the step that leads from an unmanaged collection to a collection where a professional in collections care has taken the lead. During the process you will have done a couple of things that break with old habits. You've thrown stuff away, you reorganized the storage, you restricted the access. All these necessary steps can lead to interpersonal conflicts. It is not always intuitive why one should change habits. If there is room in the collections storage area and I desperately need a place to put some chairs, why shouldn't I put them there? If there are still rats and mice in the storage room, why am I not allowed to drink my coke there? We've always rehearsed in the collections room on Saturday evenings, me and my band, why can't we keep on doing this?

You can't avoid running into a couple of difficult discussions while managing a collection. However, explaining why one does the things one does makes it often easier to understand. That's why it might be a good idea to invite the people you work with for a guided tour through the newly organized spaces when you are done with reorganizing. This gives you the chance to explain why you did things in a certain way and why it has to stay that way. It also gives the people who have access to the institution the opportunity to ask questions about things they don't understand and provide feedback about what they think should be done differently. Keep in mind that while policies are necessary to define working processes, most people don't like to read them. This guided tour provides a unique opportunity to win people over for your collections policy. For example, you can show what efforts have to be made to research ownership because there was no policy for the accession process. That's much easier to understand than the written word.

You might even invite upper management to this tour or for a second tour. This will not only open up the opportunity to show off what you've achieved so far but also to point out the most crucial issues that need funding.

THE SECOND LOGICAL EXIT

At this logical exit you should have

- a room or building where you can name the location of every object you find.
- distinct places for working with the collection, as well as places for storage materials, tools, eating, and trash.
- the biggest issues with the collection storage space or area fixed, at least in a rough-and-ready way.
- controlled access to the storage area or at least a plan of how to control the access.
- explained the new organization to the people you work with and maybe to upper management in a guided tour.

This second logical exit is also one where roads might part. If the collection is stored in a place that is not too bad, you can proceed with the next steps.

However, there are situations that are so bad that continuing with the next steps means wasting time and achieving nothing. Take the mold example one more time: to work on a collection infested with mold you and/or a conservator need to check and treat every object to remove the mold. If the mold is caused by the climate in the storage room (which is most likely) and this can't be changed (which is also very likely) you need to have a better storage room to move the collection objects to after treatment. If you haven't, it doesn't make any sense to start working with the collection. You should concentrate all your efforts on finding a better storage space.

If your working environment is in a condition a doctor would call "good, considering the circumstances," it's finally time to dive into your collection and figure out what you will be working on in the future.

NOTES

1. When working with a collection that contains a variety of hazardous chemicals like those in a medical history museum or a historical drugstore, you should bring in an expert to check as soon as possible. In addition, there are the Safety Data Sheets (SDS) that you can get for all potentially harmful substances. You can find all publications by the Occupational Safety & Health Administration (OSHA) on this website: https://www.osha.gov/pls/publications/publication.html. You might like to make yourself familiar with the "Globally Harmonized System of Classification and Labeling of Chemicals (GHS)" by the United Nations. It recommends certain international, standardized pictographs and labeling methods that will help to see what makes a certain item dangerous and will make communication with disposal experts easier. Because it will tell future staff how to handle an item, labeling in accordance with the GHS system is even recommended for the items that contain hazardous substances, but will be accessioned. You will find the latest revision of the GHS on the website of the United Nations Economic Commission for Europe (UNECE): http://www.unece.org/trans/danger/publi/ghs/ghs_welcome_e.html.

2. Paul Dickson, *The Official Rules: 5,427 Laws, Principles, and Axioms to Help You Cope with Crises, Deadlines, Bad Luck, Rude Behavior, Red Tape, and Attacks by Inanimate Objects* (Mineola, NY: Dover Publications, 2013), 36.

3. Darlene Bialowski, e-mail to the author, April 4, 2015.

Chapter Five

Diving into the Collection

With your working place set up and, if you are lucky, already granted some money to buy some materials, you are now finally ready to dive into the collection and start working with it. It is tempting to start with anything that appeals to you or with something that seems to be an easy, complete, manageable part of the collection. But there are three reasons why this isn't a good approach:

1. As long as you haven't got an overview of all the items, you run into the danger of accessioning something that you have in better condition and/ or with a whole story around it somewhere else. When you are able to compare both pieces right from the start you will most likely decide to accession just the piece with the story and/or the better condition.
2. When a part of the collection seems easy to accession, the question is if it is wise to do it now and if it should be done by you. You still have a whole lot of work to do with the rest of the unmanaged collection, and accessioning an easy, complete, manageable collection might be a great task for a volunteer or intern if you happen to get one.
3. While you are sorting the rest of the collection, you might decide that the part of the collection that seemed to be so easy, complete, and manageable at first doesn't really fit with the rest of the collection and should be given to another institution. Sure, the other institution will profit from the time you invested into this part, but not your own collection.

So, if this approach is problematic and you risk wasting your time, what is a good approach? As painful as it is, it means that you still can't start accessioning in this step; first you have to sort your collection. Every good painter will tell you that he or she spends much more time on preparation than in ac-

Figure 5.1. Unmanaged collection with a lot of managing to do (2009), picture courtesy of Missouri State Museum, Missouri State Parks.

tually painting a room. This ensures that the paint job can be done effectively and that customers are satisfied. So, what holds true for a professional painter also holds true for the museum professional in most cases.

Note: There are three kinds of collections for which you can skip this step:

1. If your collection only consists of big, bulky things like industrial machines or furniture with no small parts at all. In this instance you can categorize the collection on paper and start with accessioning your objects following those categories.
2. If your unmanaged collection is a historic house where the rooms were left unaltered and chances are that most of the things you find should be kept because of their relationship to the house owner. In this case your approach should be the one of a good archaeologist or archivist: document room by room, closet by closet, drawer by drawer, and layer by layer.
3. If your unmanaged collection is already completely sorted into logical groups.

However, I have never encountered an unmanaged collection that didn't have at least one small portion of artifacts that needed sorting.

WHY SORTING?

I've already mentioned some points about why it is problematic to just start "anywhere," but why exactly is sorting so important?

In the first place, it helps to get an overview of the whole collection. Through sorting you meet your objects face-to-face. You will discover connections between objects, such as when you find the missing dough hook of the food processor you just sorted with the kitchen equipment or the childhood drawing that shows the whole family with the new food processor. You will get an idea of what the strong points of your collection are—the things that make it outstanding and unique. You will discover great stories. Maybe there are objects in remarkably good condition, which makes them outstanding.

You will also discover the weak points of your collection. You might discover through sorting that there are categories you are just not able to fill with many significant objects. This might lead in return to an adjustment of your collections policy. You might discover objects with huge condition issues that need immediate action or that have to be removed from the collection. Sorting will also help you discover issues that weren't obvious so far, such as hidden infestations with mold or pests or hazardous substances. But there's much more to it.

Sorting makes it easier to spot duplicates and things that don't fit into the scope of your collection. If you have defined a collections policy as recommended in chapter 3, this opens up the possibility to gain more space pretty soon. For example, if you gather all tools in an old locksmith shop, you will most likely end up with sets of tools that are complete and others that are missing something. There is strong evidence that the complete set of wrenches should be accessioned. But what about single wrenches that are duplicates of the ones in the complete set?

As a trained museum professional you might feel a strong reluctance to giving something away, as somehow everything in this locksmith's shop belongs together. This is good, but keep in mind that if you define "belonging together" too widely you might end up keeping everything because everything in the world belongs together somehow. You are in the process of improving the collection and that means the things you actually accession need proper care in the future—which means investing in storage and packaging as well as staff time for care. Deciding carefully what to keep and what not to keep means caring for the collection as a whole. A single wrench that duplicates the one in the complete set will most likely not hold any additional information, thus won't add value to the collection as a whole. On the other hand, space you gain through objects you don't keep adds value for the collection because you gain space for installing storage furniture in order to better store the collection.

It will depend on your situation what you do with those duplicates, as well as with other things you feel shouldn't be accessioned. It's always safest to follow the deaccession procedure you've defined in your collections policy, but of course there are always exceptions to this rule: the original owner of the collections might have defined in his or her will that objects that are deemed not fitting for the collection should be given to a certain charity organization, or the owner of a certain artifact might have made a restricted gift with the requirement that the artifact has to be returned if it isn't accessioned. Whatever you decide to do, giving it to another museum, returning it to the original owner, or throwing it away, be sure to document the process so that future colleagues know what happened.

Another advantage of sorting is that it helps to design the next working processes more smoothly. Documenting things that are alike saves time. The obvious reason is that you can copy and paste some of the information—although this is not always recommended because of the high risk of copying mistakes. The not-so-obvious reason is that you gain knowledge about the objects that you can apply to the other objects. When you accession similar objects you have learned the terminology and right nomenclature by heart in no time, a process that doesn't take place if you accession diversified objects. To stay with the example: when you have learned that it is a "wrench, crescent," you will know it when you accession the next one some hours later, after a whole lot of other wrenches like "wrench, key" and "wrench, tap," but you won't know it weeks later after accessioning totally different items [1].

Sorting is also the starting point to assign tasks to others, like volunteers, interns, or assistant staff members, who are able to help you with the collection. "Accession square B3" is not a very effective task to assign to someone. "Accession this collection of metalworking tools" will produce much better results. Your assistant might still need to ask you some things, but given the similarity of items, there is a high chance that he or she can work independently after the first few questions. As a big plus, this person will most likely become an expert for this special area of your collection—an invaluable asset for later exhibitions, marketing efforts, and research requests.

HOW TO SORT

The issue with sorting is that it consumes space, and space is something that you never sufficiently have. That's why you probably have to sort in several sorting steps. Actually, they more resemble waves than steps. You have to

Figure 5.2.   A collection well sorted, ready to move to a better storage space (2010), picture courtesy of Missouri State Museum, Missouri State Parks.

spread part of the collection on a table or some other place to sort it, then condense it again by packing it, then spread it again to do another, more detailed sorting, which eventually is followed by more condensing and sorting phases. That's why I will refer to this process as "waves" further on.

For this process you will need some supplies. I already mentioned tables, and it helps a great deal if you have some shelving units. You can do without these, but what you definitely need are boxes. They don't have to be archival boxes (although, of course, it doesn't hurt if they are) but they have to be clean. If you haven't any boxes, read chapter 9, "We Had Nothing," and go find some.

If you are lucky, the collection is already roughly sorted into categories—all the TV sets are in one room and all the radios are in the other. If you are not so lucky, there is no recognizable form of categorization done by your predecessors. If it is the average unmanaged or partly managed collection you will most likely find a mixture of roughly sorted and not sorted items. Normally someone has started to categorize and sometimes even cataloged the collection meticulously but wasn't able to follow it through, so you have

Figure 5.3.   A well-managed collection in its new storage area (2015), picture courtesy of Missouri State Museum, Missouri State Parks.

found organized parts of the collection but also heaps or piles of boxes that contain stuff belonging to different categories. If you have this kind of collection, you will immediately understand why it is so important to reach logical exits and to write a summary or journal of the work done with the collection thus far. If you only knew what your predecessors were thinking when they stopped and why.

To start sorting effectively, you have to define categories for your sorting process. Generally speaking there are three systems in categorization:

- subject based: a categorization system based on logical topics. If you have already written your collections policy it should be rather easy to define superordinate categories that encompass a whole range of objects and subordinate categories that divide this range into smaller portions. For example, in a farming collection you might categorize into the different tasks in the fields and around the house. Your category "Cultivation of Grain" might hold the subcategories "Sowing," "Cultivating," "Reaping," "Soil Improvement," and maybe "Machinery Maintenance." Another possible form of subject-based categorization might include periods or eras—to stay in the example, "Farming in the 19th Century," "Farming before WWI," "Farming between WWI and WWII," and "Farming after WWII." If you haven't written your collections policy so far, now is a good time to do it.
- material based: a categorization system based on different materials needing different care. A material-based categorization considers the environmental needs like temperature, relative humidity, and light.
- size based: a categorization system based on objects of different sizes requiring different handling and storing. A box with photographs can be easily moved and stored on a shelf, tools and machinery might require handling aids, and some heavy machines and vehicles might require special equipment like forklifts, trucks, or cranes.

All sorting and storing processes will sooner or later consider all three of these aspects, but in the beginning one of them has to take the lead.

In many unmanaged collections with less than ideal storage conditions it's best to start with a material-based system. Define what materials suffer the most damage due to the current storage conditions and consider the options to do something about them. For example, in a shed that is freezing cold in winter and hot in the summer, all the objects suffer. But the tractors, plows, and scythes made of metal and wood will survive this situation a bit longer than photographs, documents, and textiles. Having spotted the most delicate materials, the next question is: Do you have the means to care for them properly? You either have to find a better storage room for them in your institution or look for other institutions or people who can provide appropriate care.

The matter is further complicated if you didn't have the time to go through them with due diligence so far, so you can't tell if and how much of this collection is significant to your institution and should be preserved. This is the time for collaboration. Reach out to experts in your area. Are there archives or institutions with textile collections in your area? Ask them for help. Some might be able to take over the collection you can't provide care for, others might have ideas on how you can store it for a certain period, until you can work on it and find better storage conditions. Read chapter 6, "The Power of Coffee," for more.

Seldom does size-based sorting take the lead, but it can happen. If your collection includes only a few objects that are huge, need special equipment to handle, and take up a lot of space that you desperately need for improving storage of other, smaller objects, it is again time to question whether your institution is the right place for them. For example, if there are a few vintage cars in your farming collection, consider if they are really crucial for the mission of your institution and your collection. Vintage cars need very intensive care and there are museums that specialize in them. Maybe one is willing to take the cars for their collection. Conversely, if you have a large collection of vintage cars and spare parts and discover a collection of the collector's wife's cups, saucers, and plates in the garage, you will definitely need another storage space for them, and maybe this collection doesn't fit into your institution's mission at all.

Now to subject-based sorting, which you will reach sooner or later. There are some rules to this process you have to keep in mind:

1. The narrower the categorization, the less likely you need to have a next sorting step and the more likely you can start accessioning in the next step.
2. The narrower the categorization, the earlier you have small, manageable units you can assign to someone else for accessioning.
3. The narrower the categorization the more space you need for sorting.
4. The narrower the categorization, the slower the sorting process.

It is a balancing act to find what is right in the given situation. I found that it's almost preferable to start each project with a few rough categories that are easy to determine and take the risk of having a second or even third step of sorting. The main reason is that you quickly get an overview and find hidden issues fast. You reduce the risk of something deteriorating unnoticed while you try to decide if some tool is for woodworking or metalworking. Speaking of that, there is a high risk of losing yourself in deciding what something is.

A REAL-WORLD EXAMPLE

We acquired a large collection of promotional items at the TECHNO-SEUM in 2011. Over a period of forty years, a collector had collected everything promotional—from small pens with a company logo to a six-foot-high inflatable milk box. The collector himself estimated his collection to hold about 3,000 items, but it turned out there were many more. The collection was stored in countless banana boxes and packing cases in three different rooms at the collector's house and moving it was a story in itself. To make it manageable we had to sort it.

Our first sorting was material and size based. We first took all large stuffed animals, because they were easy to spot and had to go to conservation for moth treatment. A few other huge items were sorted out and stored separately. These were accessioned immediately because it was clear we would keep them. We also took out things like stickers and brochures that we considered to be better stored in our archives. Then began the long journey of sorting, which needed a considerable amount of space and time. Here, our sorting was mainly subject based. We tried to define categories that made sense to us like "key chains," "clocks," or "egg cups." The occasional small stuffed animals and other textiles were sorted out and went for preventive moth treatment first and were stored separately. In the sorting process we realized that there were some companies with a wide range of promotional items, so we added categories like "BigBurger, Inc." or "The Cool Brown Beverage Company." We repacked the items in standard packing cases and ended up with ten palettes, each with about nine packing cases.

Looking back, the decision to add companies as categories caused conflicts. It helped us speeding up the sorting process because you didn't have to be an expert in promotional history to spot an item from "The Cool Brown Beverage Company," which meant that every high school intern could be assigned with the task of sorting the next few banana boxes. But it also led to similar objects being sorted into different categories. While one person decided a key chain depicting a bottle of the company belonged in the "key chains" category, the next decided that it belonged to "The Cool Brown Beverage Company" category. The issue with this didn't become obvious until later in the process.

We started accessioning the items category-wise, which meant that different staff members and interns could work on the accessioning at the same time. Given the history of the collection, there were a considerable number of duplicates and we defined right from the start the reason why we would keep duplicates—and how many of them. But given the nature of our sorting process this was hard to control. The colleague who accessioned "The Cool Brown Beverage Company" accessioned three similar key chains and threw the remaining ones away. The colleague who accessioned "key chains" did the same—with the similar key chains. So we ended up with six similar key chains. As soon as we realized this, we knew there was a further issue: every colleague had to search the database before he decided if something got accessioned. A small effort, but with more than 3,000 artifacts, a considerable time factor.

Instead, create a category "I have no idea" where you put that thing and to which you can come back later to do in-depth research.[2]

As I said in the beginning, sorting with space restrictions means sorting in "waves." That's what you need the boxes for. Make sure you find clean, sturdy boxes that can be stacked safely at least two or three high. This is easier to achieve with boxes of a standard size, but sometimes you don't have that choice. However, make sure that the boxes can hold the weight and avoid overloading the boxes. Be aware that in an environment with high humidity, cardboard boxes don't hold as much weight as when in a dry room. Needless to say you should avoid storing your collection in a climate that leads to soaked-through boxes, however, if you have to deal with this issue, avoid stacking cardboard boxes at all because you risk that the weight of the upper boxes might destroy the boxes below them—and the objects stored inside. If items are too big to be sorted into boxes, find other ways to sort them: assign certain areas of the room, for example. Make sure you mark both boxes and areas and document how you sorted and why.

What I mean by "sorting in waves" is the following: Given the restricted space you have you might start with a certain number of boxes for different categories. Let's say you have six boxes for six categories. As you sort, some of the boxes will become full and have to be replaced by empty ones. You want to stack the filled boxes on pallets, but at the moment you don't have space for six or more palettes. So you start stacking the boxes on just one palette. This means your first palette contains nine mixed boxes, for example three of "category 1," two of "category 2," two of "category 3," none of "category 4," one of "category 5" and one of "category 6." This doesn't matter at the moment, because in the process of sorting you have gained space for another palette, which is filled in the same "chaotic" way. When you are through with sorting the items into boxes you sort the palettes so that every palette only holds boxes from one category. You might now start accessioning the objects by category or start the next wave of sorting them into finer categories.

THE DANGER OF SORTING

Make no mistake, sorting holds a certain amount of danger. Namely, the danger of destroying correlations between objects. When you took the first glimpse of your collection as described in chapter 2, you took a lot of pictures and tried to keep your hands off the objects for exactly that reason, to leave the relationship one object has with other objects undisturbed. However, now you have entered the "hands-on" stage of the process and you can't avoid the risk of overlooking some connection completely. That's why it is wise to keep on taking pictures of your working process. You might not realize that one part belongs to a certain machine but if you have a picture of how it was stored when you first started sorting, you might be able to reestablish the connection later.

A REAL-WORLD EXAMPLE

I was sorting through the remains of the big collections move of the Landesmuseum für Technik und Arbeit in 2006. Among the objects with unknown identity – either because they had lost their label or because they had made it into the museum's storage without ever being accessioned – I discovered a small tin pot. Nothing spectacular, it just looked like every ordinary tin can. When I looked at the bottom I discovered the manufacturer's mark reading "Eicke 2".

That's when I realized what I had in my hands. It was a tin pot belonging to a certain kind of coffee maker that was manufactured in Germany around 1900. They were sold with fitting tin pot but most of the time the coffee maker and tin pot became separated over time. The coffee maker was sold or thrown away while the tin pot was reused for other purposes. We had a few "Eicke" coffee makers in our collection, but none had its tin pot. We even had an "Eicke 2" coffee maker. Chances are the pot and the machine became separated when they were already in the museum, probably when the large collection of coffee makers and mills that contained our "Eicke 2" was sorted.

Figure 5.4. The tin pot marked "Eicke 2", accession number EVZ:2012/0244, TECHNOSEUM, Foto Hans Bleh

Figure 5.5. Newspaper ad for the coffee maker "Eicke" taken from "Fliegende Blätter Nr. 2050" from 1884

It was the sheer luck that I once was working for another project searching old magazines for coffee maker advertisements for an exhibition that made the name "Eicke" ring a bell in my head.

Otherwise it only would have been any old single tin pot to me and I probably would have suggested deaccessioning it because tin pots were not in the scope of our collections.

THE THIRD LOGICAL EXIT

When you are finished with sorting you have reached the next logical exit. You have sorted the collection into logical categories and documented how you have decided on the categorization and why. Now you are in the position to actually start accessioning your collection. But before that, a few words on the power of networking and collaboration, I call it the "Power of Coffee."

NOTES

1. All nomenclatures taken from: Paul Bourcier and Ruby Rogers, ed., *Nomenclature 3.0 for Museum Cataloging: Robert G. Chenhall's System for Classifying Cultural Objects.* (Lanham, MD: AltaMira Press, 2010), 183.

2. At the TECHNOSEUM we actually have a whole row of shelving units called "The X-Shelves" for those objects that we either don't know what they are or are not sure if they have just lost their accession number or were never accessioned. Whenever time allows, a colleague works through these objects, researches what they are and if they can be found in the files, and continues with accessioning or deaccessioning them. Note: Originally, we didn't have the TV series "The X-Files" in mind, it was just that we numbered the rows alphabetically and the last row was the twenty-fourth and therefore got the *X*.

Chapter Six

The Power of Coffee

It's funny: history museums are about humans. History is formed by the interaction of people, in the best and in the worst sense of the word. Our collections are stuffed with objects that were collected because of human relationships. Objects were kept because they reminded someone of somebody; later they were deemed worth the effort of keeping because they were related to somebody or some occasion in history. And, in your case, somebody decided that this collection has to be brought to a managed state. Through a whole series of human interactions it's now your job to manage this collection.

Yet, when we look at professional museum literature we find that the human aspect of the actual work is left out. Somehow, we assume that while we know that there is a human aspect in everything that we do, it is not "professional" to mention it in trade books, or we assume that these aspects have to be isolated and talked about in books about psychology or human resource management. While I understand the reasoning behind it, I will break with this custom. You are thrown into the task of managing an unmanaged collection and I promised in the beginning that I will talk you through the process step-by-step. One important step is to understand the human relationships that are important for managing an unmanaged collection. In fact, it's not a step; it's a constant consideration of human needs and human relationships that help to manage your collection.

CREATING GREAT CONSTELLATIONS

It's a truism that the more money you invest into collections care, the better you are able to do preventive conservation and the more likely you will save the collection for future generations. However, there are always examples of small institutions that seem to have few possibilities, yet reach better results in collections care than many larger institutions. When you look closer you will always find an amazing constellation of people. I say "constellation" on purpose, because it doesn't necessarily need to be the classical team of museum professionals and it often isn't. You'll find everything from a highly flexible board with a creative executive director, to a group of volunteers that decides there is a need to bring their collection to the highest possible professional standards. You'll find some examples of great constellations in chapter 11, "Success Stories."

Those constellations always need a certain amount of luck. The right people at the right place at the right time. But while luck is certainly involved, there is much that can be done in working toward creating a good constellation. The difficulty is that it does not have much to do with what we usually understand when referring to the term "work." The closest term to this idea is "networking," but this is an overused buzzword that is often interpreted in a way that doesn't cover the aspects that are really important. What I am talking about has to do with getting involved with the people who are connected to your collection—people who can help you with your actual work, as well as people who are important as advocates and supporters of your collection. It's about sharing what you do to make people understand what makes your work important and your collection unique. It's also about learning what is important to the people in your community—may it be politicians, school teachers, firefighters, policemen, donors, craftspeople, or local shop owners.

I call this concept the "Power of Coffee" because I can positively say that I learned more things, solved more problems, and made more connections by talking to people over a cup of coffee (or a piece of cake or a glass of beer) than in formal meetings. The reason for this is strikingly simple: in a formal meeting we have a reason why we are meeting and we focus on this reason. In general this is a good thing because we want to reach results. But the formal reason for the meeting keeps us focused on a single topic and prevents us from seeing other aspects of the constellation at hand. We all have great troubleshooting abilities, but we normally only use them for problems that directly affect ourselves or people we care for. That's why we sometimes forget to use them in a formal environment like a professional meeting.

Here's a scenario to illustrate this concept: In the process of storage planning, you schedule a meeting with the chief of the local fire department, a city official, and an architect. All parties know why they are there and will act in the role for which they were invited to attend the meeting. The fire chief will look at the plans to point out everything that is against safety regulations, the city official will point out what to keep in mind to stay in accordance with the overall development plan, and the architect will try to align his plans to these requirements or argue for different solutions. Everybody acts as a professional, but only with the part of his or her professional self that is good at pointing out real or potential issues. The part of the professional self that is good at troubleshooting and at seeing possible solutions is not in active mode. That's quite natural, because the topic of this meeting seems only to require the problem-spotting mode. So, let's say the debate gets heated over the width of the fire lane that leads to the storage annex of the museum building. The fire chief points out that the architect's current plans do not reflect the required width. The architect points out that it doesn't because access is blocked on one side by parts of a monumental stone sculpture that was accessioned by the museum years ago and never got reassembled in the city park as originally planned. The sculpture weighs several tons and the museum can't afford to move it, least of all reassemble it, because it can't afford the shipping experts and heavy equipment to make this happen. The architect suggests putting the fire lane on the opposite side of the building but the city official points out that this would not work because it would require building an access from another street and such a project isn't in accordance with the city's development plan. The discussion revolves around this topic and after two hours the meeting ends with the outcome that the museum and its architect have to plan something that will meet all requirements.

Let's build the same scenario, but this time we use the "Power of Coffee." Let's assume that you connected to those experts long before it was clear that there will be new storage. You met them informally, without a certain purpose in mind. You dropped by at the local fire department with a cake, the department head showed off her department's newest truck, and you had some cake and a coffee with her and her "boys." You ran into the city official after work in the local pub and you had a nice evening talking about how money is tight and how rules and regulations made it difficult to find good solutions in development planning. When you started planning, you gave the architect a storage tour and talked about conservation issues and great museum architecture over a cup of coffee afterward.

When you now schedule the same meeting about the same topic with the same experts you've built a relationship with beforehand, you have therefore increased the likeliness that each of them will look at the plans using their troubleshooting abilities. They know what's important to you and they know what the situation is. The issue is still the same: the fire lane is not the required width. But now, the fire chief says: "Wait a minute: all your trouble comes from those sculpture parts blocking the way? Could you build the lane large enough if they were removed?" It turns out that the local fire department doesn't have a crane truck, but the fire department in the next city has one. It isn't needed very often so they are always open to possibilities to use it for training. Now, if the museum finds a place to move the sculpture to, the chief offers to ask her fellow fire chief for assistance. The city official asks if there is a picture of the sculpture that he could show his boss. He offers to find a place for it on city grounds. There is a lot of planning ahead, but it seems there is a possible solution: the two fire departments moving and assembling the sculpture in a city park, solving not only the problem at hand, but also adding value by displaying the sculpture in public again.

As you see, in both scenarios the experts acted as professionals. But in the second scenario the professionals used their full troubleshooting potential. This is not to say that this kind of troubleshooting doesn't happen if you haven't met the experts in an informal context before. It does. It also doesn't mean that knowing those people better automatically leads to better solutions. It's not an inevitable process. If you don't get along well with the fire chief, no coffee and cake in the world will change that. But the "Power of Coffee" increases the likelihood of people's looking at a problem at hand with the big picture in mind. If we know what is important to someone, we are more likely to take his or her point of view and look at an issue from his or her perspective, and we are more likely to use our knowledge and experience to create possible solutions and improvements.

Keep in mind that this is not a one-way street: it's not always others who can help you by using their troubleshooting abilities. Let's continue with the same scenario: you might help the fire department by showing them how to build a more effective and easier to use file system, how to organize the department's collection of photographs, or point them to an expert in ancient fire engines to work with them caring for their beloved but decaying 1920s fire truck.

Human relationships have the biggest impact on success or failure of any endeavor. So let's take a deeper look into the relationships that are important for managing an unmanaged collection.

YOUR COMMUNITY

They say that it takes a town to raise a child and the same is true for collections care—except for the rare occasion where the collection belongs to a private collector who has no intention of making it accessible to the public. Yet after his or her death the collection may belong to a community, either in the real sense of the word or in an idealistic way. It depicts the history of a certain town, area, group, or topic that is relevant for the people that live in the vicinity of this collection. For the long-term care of a collection, it is crucial that this community understands the value and importance of the collection for their own lives. Only this understanding will insure that policies are followed and the collection is cared for even after you have finished the project or some other person has taken over.

In a large museum, there is a whole team that makes sure the community cares about the museum. There are marketing professionals, educators, development officers. Everybody does his or her job to keep the community involved so that the registrar, collections manager, or conservator can focus on collections care. In a smaller museum you have to bring together some parts of these jobs to help improve your collection.

It's not as time consuming as it seems. Most of those jobs can be done in a small community by simply being the "face" of the collection. You live in your community just as every other citizen, so you will naturally come into contact with other community members. By simply talking about what you do (leaving safety issues out of the conversation, of course), you ensure that people know that the collection exists. By talking about what issues you face you raise awareness about collections care. It's also a great way of promoting museum activities. Just tell other people about them.

If people know what you are doing they will more likely see the connections to their own lives and occupation. And the other way around, you might see the possibilities of solving an issue with your collection by working with somebody from your community. This might lead to solutions you haven't thought about before. The owner of your local computer shop might offer to give you the clean cardboard boxes the equipment is shipped in rather than throwing them away. The local scout pack decides that they will help you with your storage cleaning for their activity week. Your local quilt association decides that their annual fund-raiser will be held to benefit your collection this time. Just don't expect that these things will happen naturally. It takes a connection to a human being to understand the abstract value of a collection. You can establish this connection by being the ambassador of your collection.

YOUR PEERS

It can be daunting to be the only one caring for a historical collection for miles around. You might meet a lot of people every day, but chances are that these are not people you can discuss specialized collections issues with. Few janitors really care about nomenclature issues and your local grocery shop owner might be compassionate about your numbering conundrum but can't really provide any substantial help. That's why it is important to stay connected to other collections professionals.

A REAL-WORLD EXAMPLE

Years ago we accepted a donation of tools and materials from a circa 1910 funeral parlor. Along with a horse-drawn, glass-sided hearse, and really (really!) scary tools was a glass jar marked "Thoracic Fluid." The rubber stopper had swelled to completely seal the bottle, preventing evaporation. Still sloshing around inside was about an inch of clearish liquid. We had some skepticism about the actual contents but had no way of identifying it short of opening the bottle.

Wanting to keep the bottle but not the contents, I started making calls. No public safety entity—police, fire department, hazmat—would open the bottle without knowing the contents. They would only destroy the bottle completely. The director of a funeral facility was equally reluctant. He did tell me that if the contents was a simple formaldehyde solution, I could pour it down the drain!

As a long shot, my museum director called the Iowa Bureau of Criminal Investigation (IBCI), across the street from my museum. They were thrilled to take on the problem of the Thoracic Fluid bottle! In their lab, I watched five gloved and masked techs place the bottle in a fume hood and gently pry the stopper out. One tech dipped a finger into the liquid and sniffed. I do believe there was some disappointment when the liquid turned out to be a weak formaldehyde solution and not an actual body fluid.

It was a win-win: I kept the intact bottle for the collection and IBCI got to practice their forensic skills.

Jodene K. Evans
Registrar
State Historical Museum, Iowa

One way to do this is to stay connected with professional organizations like the American Alliance of Museums (AAM) and its Registrars Committee (RCAAM), the American Association of State and Local History (AASLH), the Association of Registrars and Collections Specialists (ARCS), or the museum association of your state or region. Through them you will have opportunities to stay up-to-date with workshops, courses, and conferences, and you can find out who the other museums and collections specialists are in your area. Often, collections in the same area face the same challenges—like climate issues or natural catastrophes—and therefore have developed strategies for how to deal with them. Reach out to those colleagues to swap stories and get information. Sometimes this opens up other possibilities, like joining together in buying archival equipment to claim a quantity discount. Sometimes larger institutions need to get rid of old crates or storage equipment and you can get them for free or a bargain price. Connecting to institutions the same size as yours is invaluable for exchanging experiences—for example, learning about how good a database software is for small-museum purposes.

Subscribing to professional discussions, like the listserv of the Registrars Committee of the American Alliance of Museums (http://www.rcaam.org/Listserv) helps you to stay up-to-date with developments in the field. It's also a great resource to post questions on when in doubt. Staying informed about what happens in the field is important because standards in collections care might change due to more recent studies, laws might change, and there might be new grants available that could be relevant for your collection.

For feeling less like a lone wolf with a weird job, there is nothing better than meeting other museum professionals. Try reaching out to other museums in your town or area and get together over a cup of coffee or any other preferred drink every now and then. Exchanging thoughts and swapping horror stories is a great way to keep you psychologically healthy and your feet on the ground.

YOUR STAFF

When you read this subheading your immediate response is probably the one introduced by Bob Beatty in the preface to *Stewardship: Collections and Historic Preservation*: "Hey, *I'm* my staff."[1] Yes, you probably are in the common sense of the word. You may be the only museum professional for the next 500 miles, the single volunteer museum director, or the student assistant to the assistant curator with absolutely no power in the hierarchy of your institution. However, you are responsible for the collection and that means you are in a way responsible for those who work with the collection. It's you who knows the collection, it's you who knows which items contain hazardous material, and it's you who knows what needs to be done next to improve the collection. This means that whoever works with this collection relies on your advice, warnings, and instructions.

To get the work done you might have the chance to get an intern or two. Community members might offer to volunteer their time helping you. You might have the chance to collaborate with retired staff or people who helped building the collection. No, they are not "staff" in the true sense of the word, but you have to structure their work, advise them on how to do it, and meet their needs just like every other "boss."

This is not an introduction to the basics of human resources management. But as the so-called "soft facts" are often crucial for the success of a project, it's necessary to give this aspect some thoughts. The key is to understand what motivates people and to find out what they are good at. When you get a new colleague, you might need to work a few days or even weeks together with him or her on different tasks until you have found out what his or her strengths and weaknesses are. There are some people who know right from the start just what they want to do and what they are good at. However, often it is not that clear—especially if your new intern or volunteer has never worked in a museum. During the time you teach him or her about the dos and don'ts of collections work, you should try to get an idea of what seems to inspire or interest this individual. We all work best if we get something to do we really like to do.

In larger museums with a highly organized, "best practice" collection, the tasks you can actually assign to interns or volunteers are often very limited and clearly defined. Most of the time you will need someone with great attention to detail who loves database work. If you happen to get an intern with a different skill set, you will have difficulties finding appropriate tasks to use their skill set in your area and you probably will have to send him or her to a different department. In an unmanaged collection nearly every skill is welcome: great housekeeping abilities, creativity in building temporary storage furniture and crates, detailed knowledge about a certain object group, a love for sorting and organizing, the unique "sales" ability of talking people into donating money, IT knowledge for choosing, creating and/or maintaining a database, social media knowledge to raise support for the collection via the Internet. The possibilities are endless.

The lesson I've learned over the years of working with different colleagues is simple, yet striking: you can't handle people as if they are all the same. If someone struggles with a task you assigned to him or her it might be that you've failed in explaining it, or it might be that you've chosen something he or she isn't good at. If it's the first reason, you have to improve your training. If it's the second reason, you have to find out what tasks better suit his or her talents. That he or she isn't good at one task almost certainly means he or she is good at something else, and if you find out what it is, all benefit from it: your colleague, yourself, and the collection.

But while it is a fault to generalize about people, it is also true that different groups of people have different needs. That's why I have included a few thoughts about the needs of three groups you will most likely have to deal with: interns, volunteers, and veteran staff.

A REAL-WORLD EXAMPLE

During my time as a collections manager at the TECHNOSEUM, I have worked with a couple of amazing student assistants and apprentices.[1] Their skills were quite varied but somehow they always fit in. One was extremely good at spotting issues. When there was one database entry wrong in a whole set of 1,022 entries, he'd spot it. Same with storage issues like leaking water pipes. He had a nose for it and I could rest assured that if there was something wrong in the storage area, he'd find and report it right away. One was talented in building custom boxes for artifacts; whatever she built it was fitting and practical, as well as downright beautiful. Another was an amazing organizer; he was really good at finding what hampered logistics and coming up with solutions for it. And still another was extremely good at understanding the architecture and power of our database and at the same time was able to explain it to others who were not so good at it. I called her the "Database Whisperer."

I never considered "being nice" as a special skill until I had a student assistant who was just that: a really nice person. One could send her to the grumpiest veteran staff member to talk him into something he didn't want to do, and she managed it with grace. You could team her up with literally anyone. It was not something she practiced for, like a salesman smile; she was nice in such a natural and honest way that few people could say "no" to her.

Note

1. I use "apprentice" for the German term "Volontär." The "Volontariat" is a form of apprenticeship in the museum sector in Germany. This apprenticeship is intended for people who have majored in history, art history, or other relevant disciplines to learn the nuts and bolts of museum work. The apprenticeship contract runs for one or two years; apprentices are normally paid half of a curator's salary.

I use "student assistant" for the German term "Studentische Hilfskraft." These assistants normally study a discipline related to the museum field and work a few hours a month for the museum, in a collections department, and normally as an assistant to a curator, registrar, or collections manager.

I don't mention names because there were so many great colleagues that I would probably overlook one who would be disappointed not to be mentioned.

Interns

I use "interns" as an umbrella term for a whole range of jobs that can be found at institutions. They may be called student assistants, student helpers, junior assistants, apprentices, or in fact interns. Their positions may be paid or unpaid, and their work for an institution, like a museum, might be required by their study guidelines or done with the intent to gain practical experience in a chosen field. As varied as the reasons and job titles may be, there are a few facts that unite them: most are young to middle-aged adults who are currently studying or have the intention of studying something that is related to history or art history, and they want to start a career in the museum field or related fields in the future.

It's important to understand that you are working with a young, emerg ing professional. This individual might lack knowledge and experience, but brings in the enthusiasm of someone who sees his or her future in the museum field. This gives you the opportunity to train and be part of the career development of this person. In an ideal constellation this can result in a mentor/ mentee relationship and a lifelong professional exchange. But even if it's just a "normal" internship, you should be aware of the fact that you might have an impact on the future of this individual. This emerging professional wants and needs to learn the nuts and bolts of museum work and assisting on an unmanaged collection provides great possibilities for this.

What you have to keep in mind is that nowadays it is extremely important to do something in an internship that will look good on one's resume. What a young emerging museum professional will need the most is something that will make him or her stick out of the masses of competitors for entry level positions. Although you will have a whole lot of "brainless" tasks you just need to have done and some tasks for which you will just need a second pair of eyes and helping hands, make sure that there are a few tasks that will look good and interesting on the resume of your intern. These types of tasks might at first not be obvious, so here are a few examples:

• Working on a self-contained part of the collection makes a better project than assisting you on the whole collection. Examine your collection while sorting (see chapter 5, "Diving into the Collection") for such parts that can be easily assigned to an intern and can be done in his or her tenure. "Cleaning, researching, and documenting the tools of a locksmith's shop," or "Creating an inventory of kitchen utensils in accordance with Nomenclature 3.0," will sound much better on a resume than "assisting with documenting a farming collection"—although in principle the intern had performed the same tasks.

- Look for possibilities to give your intern some "showtime," something that is published and/or visible in public with his or her name on it. The possibilities are varied and depend on your institution: a blog post, an article in the membership newsletter, a lecture about a discovery made while doing the research. Discuss this with your intern; you might end up with an innovative idea that is a win for all sides—like publishing ancient cooking recipes on the museum website.
- Collections work is a—if not *the*—foundation of museum work. However, give your intern the opportunity to look at other fields of museum work. In a larger museum, talk to the other departments to see if they need help for a certain project or event. In a small museum you will have a whole range of tasks with which you'll need help, so it shouldn't be a problem to assign to your intern something like the planning of a lecture or guiding a tour. If you have just the collection to deal with, you can assign to your intern the task of getting creative. Maybe he or she sees a possibility to improve the outreach and public awareness for the collection.

Sometimes colleagues who are trained museum professionals fear they are raising future competition by training interns. This is true, but the fact is that this competition for museum jobs is there anyway, whether you do a good or bad job training your intern. I would like to provide another way to look at it: When you provide the best possible training you increase the likeliness that this young professional secures a good job in the business and makes a decent career. And there's nothing better than knowing there's someone in another museum who owes you a big one.

Volunteers

Volunteers are a varied group, the group you may most likely make wrong assumptions about when you try to capture what they have in common. Some volunteers are well over seventy and chose to volunteer because they feel they should pass on their knowledge to younger people before it's too late. Others are young and volunteer in a museum to gain experiences or stay in training on their chosen career path. And others of all ages volunteer because they feel an obligation to contribute to the cultural heritage of their community. You have to find out and address those different motivations that come along with different expectations about volunteering.

The absolute best way to find out what motivates your volunteer is to talk with each of them. Don't make it a formal job interview, for it isn't (and most job interviews are terrible situations anyway, but that's a different story). Sit down over a cup of coffee, tea, or whatever and talk about what the volunteer expects and what drives them to offer their free time to help you with your project. You know your collection so you might already see potential tasks while you are talking, but avoid offering special tasks too fast. Sometimes what a volunteer wishes to do is not what he or she is really good at. Sometimes you might jump too fast on the first thing the volunteer tells you they are good at, just to realize later there would have been another, more important task they would have been equally qualified for but now they don't want to switch tasks.

For younger volunteers who offer their help to stay in training, many of the things said about interns is true. For other volunteers working on a self-contained part of the collection is not as important. You can look for other tasks that need to be done and fit the expectations of your volunteer. Having an amateur or retired professional photographer might be great for taking pictures of the collection. Having a glowing housekeeper who wants to make friends with new people could be a starting point to form a "housekeeping task force" that dives into tidying the collection spaces and developing an integrated pest management procedure. Having an unemployed programmer who feels bored sitting at home playing "World of Warcraft" on his computer might be a perfect choice for working on a great website about the collection. Look at the skills your volunteer can provide and try to match those skills with the needs of the collection.

Keep in mind that these are volunteers. This means they are not motivated by money, nor can you order them to do something. Managing volunteers is a difficult task and one that needs great people skills because the only way to have them do something is to convince them that it's worth being done. That's why really good volunteer coordinators are hard to find. However, a good starting point is showing them that you appreciate that they are willing to donate their precious time. It's equally important to convey the message about why professional collections care is important and why they should apply the same high standards as paid museum professionals to their work for this collection. Make sure they understand that you are correcting them when they handle objects or do database entries, not because you want to scold them, but because you want to use best practice in collections care.

Showing appreciation is not always easy. And as your institution is probably short of money anyway, it's probably difficult to invite your volunteers for a big lunch once a year. But as you are using the "Power of Coffee," you might find other possibilities. You know the colleagues in the museums in your area, so how about reaching an agreement that the volunteers of those museum get free entry to your museum and vice versa? You can join forces asking every staff member and every volunteer in your area to bring something to eat for a joint picnic of museum people in your area. Sometimes suppliers you work with send you promotional material you can share with your volunteers. There are always possibilities if you invest some thought and creativity. And never forget that a "great idea," "good job," or "you did awesome" doesn't cost anything and—if meant seriously—is always appreciated.

Veterans

I don't use the term "veterans" in the military sense but in the sense of someone who has done a certain job for a long time. You will often encounter veterans in your job. They may be staff members, volunteers, city officials, collectors, or the janitor who holds the keys to the collections shack—but they have one thing in common: they knew the collection before you knew it and before you came. In theory that sounds like a perfect match—the knowledge of a lifetime teamed up with fresh ideas coming from current research.

However, in everyday work this relationship holds a certain amount of potential conflict and not all relationships run smoothly from the beginning. In fact, I've encountered several times when something that at first looked like a technical conflict (i.e., about what database to choose or what to catalog), turned out to be a personal conflict. This conflict was rooted in the fact that one party entered the museum work force two years after Noah's Ark was built (or at least behaves like that's the case) and the other party was a young emerging museum professional who just earned his museum studies degree. On the one side, pride of the knowledge gathered through a lifetime of experience teamed up with the presumption that this knowledge is not appreciated enough and the fear of being regarded as obsolete. And then, on the other side, the pride of the other's achievements teamed up with the presumption that these achievements are not recognized enough and the fear of not being taken seriously. The battle lines are drawn somewhere between one side saying, "We've always done it that way," "We have saved this collection from destruction before you even could spell the word 'collection,'" and "Those things were created to be in use and you make a fuss about them like they are artworks," and the other side arguing, "This place is a mess," "how can anyone who has an ounce of common sense cram objects into a room that way?" and "We will do this the way best practice suggests or we won't do it at all."

As with many personal conflicts the best way to address the issue is right from the start instead of ignoring it until it becomes a real problem. To do that, both sides have to take a look at the value each side brings to the common endeavor of managing this unmanaged collection. Here are just a few thoughts that might help to overcome prejudices and find a common basis to tackle this collection together.

As the museum professional who is new to the job keep these ideas in mind:

• Veterans have collected objects that are relevant for the mission of the institution.
• Veterans often invested time and effort in doing this, sometimes risked being laughed at by others, or even felt threatened while doing so.
• Veterans have probably acted to the best of their knowledge by doing the things they did. For example, arsenic was commonly used for preserving and treating taxidermy specimens. Cursing our predecessors for doing so ignores the fact that this was the only thing they knew they could do to keep those taxidermy specimen from being destroyed by pests.
• Veterans have gathered incredible knowledge about the objects or groups of objects in the collection—an invaluable asset for future documentation. They have probably forgotten more about the collection than the young professional will ever learn.
• Veterans have probably fought for better storage conditions but couldn't push through the resistance.
• Just because there is a hole in the roof doesn't necessarily mean nobody tried to fix it. It might be that others kept him or her from doing so.
• Veterans probably didn't know how to educate themselves about treatment of objects. Museum professionals often think that many things are common knowledge while in fact the museum business is very small and comparatively young. Many insurance agents, engineers, and farmers who form a volunteer force of a museum probably haven't heard that there's a profession for it.
• You will be regarded as a "youngster" by veterans even if you've reached your mid-fifties. For someone who can still remember having a couple of drinks with the person the historic house is dedicated to, that means you've just escaped kindergarten.

As a veteran yourself who is confronted with a young emerging museum professional keep these ideas in mind:

• People who have a degree in Museum Studies have gone through a thorough training program in collections care—most of it being not only book knowledge, but hands-on training as well.
• There is an incredibly large amount to know about collections care and, indeed, things that look harmless—like ordinary cardboard, a vinyl bag, or a common detergent—can do much harm to collections.
• Knowledge in collections care develops quickly. There is new research done every day, so what was thought of as "best practice" five years ago

might have changed by now. It's good to have someone who is up-to-date with current research.

- Young museum professionals might lack experience, but they bring a lot of energy and good ideas.
- Someone who is new to the community might see things differently. He or she might see solutions someone who grew up in the community isn't able to see just because "it has always been that way."

So, how do you address the issues at hand and the mistrust on both sides to form a really effective team of veterans and younger professionals? Well, you may have guessed it already, you use the Power of Coffee. Calling a formal meeting will probably lead to an awkward situation: The museum professional outlining the project on a whiteboard like a teacher and the veteran staff sitting there like students and waiting for the professional to say something stupid or do something wrong. Almost every time, the better way is to find a more informal setting to talk to each other. Coffee and a piece of cake in the break room, lunch at a nearby restaurant, or a stroll in the city park. Get to know each other. Talk about what is important to you and what is important to the collection. Veterans might tell stories about how the collection developed and how the stage you see now was reached; you might encounter that this is actually a major improvement from what it was ten years ago. The young professional might talk about his or her studies and experiences in other museums. Try everything to make it a situation all members feel comfortable with. Don't choose the local pub for talking if it is notorious for being the domain of all the old men in the community. Don't choose the city park if it's a loud place where all the youngsters play music and scream and you can't hear yourself speak. Choose a neutral place where everyone can relax.

THE POWER OF HUMAN RELATIONSHIPS

You've seen by reading this chapter that human relationships have a considerable impact on the success of managing a previously unmanaged collection. Good relationships with officials, board members, and donors are crucial for all the things you need to improve the condition of the collection. Good relationships with your fellow colleagues will keep you up-to-date and mentally supported. Good relationships in your everyday working environment and—if you are lucky to have one—team are crucial for getting things done within a tight budget. But you need to acknowledge that human relationships take time to build and nurture. Finding assistance for your unmanaged collection won't be easy and dream teams don't fall from the sky. Not everyone will get along and some working relationships will always be tense. In fact, many later dream teams didn't start off as such, but developed by getting to know each other, exchanging different points of view, addressing issues, and sometimes leading challenging discussions. Forming a team of people who think and act alike is never a good approach. In the worst case scenario, this leads to a uniform "group think" that might accept and blindly follow wrong solutions because no one is daring to think differently and speak up. The key is having a common goal—here, the managing of an unmanaged collection—and taking advantage of experience, availability, youth, interest, and creativity that everyone brings to the equation. Try your best to create a good working environment in which you work toward dismantling existing prejudices and establishing a culture of respect. On the basis of good human relationships, you will be able to achieve incredible things.

NOTE

1. Bob Beatty, preface to *Stewardship: Collections and Historic Preservation*, Book 6, *Small Museum Toolkit*, edited by Cinnamon Catlin-Legutko and Stacy Klingler (Lanham, MD: AltaMira Press, 2012), xii.

Chapter Seven

Getting Stuff Done

In chapter 5 we sorted our collection and maybe you sorted it several additional times until you now have it at a stage where you can actually start the accessioning process. It's a good thing that you've dealt with your collection, as this means that you have gotten yourself acquainted with it. You know its strengths and weaknesses and you have a rough idea of how many objects you are dealing with. This knowledge is important, because you have to make some strategic decisions now.

Much is written about the process of accessioning and how to catalog a collection. For a start, read *Object Entry Procedure, Acquisition Procedure* and *Cataloguing Procedure* of *Spectrum 4.0*[1] and Daniel Reibel's *Registration Methods for the Small Museum.*[2] While reading this literature will give you a good idea of what's important in the next step, the material doesn't relieve you of the duty of considering your current situation and setting up a strategic plan specific to how you'll approach the documentation process of your collection.[3]

With the risk of stating the obvious, here are some rules that are inevitable truisms of object documentation:

1. The more detailed the cataloging, the more time it takes to do it.
2. The more detailed the cataloging, the more useful it is for research, curating, education, and any other object use.
3. Objects that are physically there but can not be found in documentation are "invisible" for any object use.
4. The longer the documentation of a single object takes, the longer it takes until the whole collection is documented and the longer objects stay "invisible."

5. It is actually possible to create a completely useless catalog by being too generic and vague in naming objects in favor of saving time or by not cataloging facts that are crucial for further steps in the process. The objects are then "visible"—but still useless.

As you see, you are running into a set of conflicting rules as you previously had in "How to Sort" in chapter 5 when you had to decide how narrow your categorization would be. Only the decision you have to make now has much more impact on the future use of your collection.

LAYING OUT A DOCUMENTATION STRATEGY

You can boil this decision down to these questions: How much data per single object do I really need? What data do I have to record now because it will be lost otherwise? What can be researched later and/or by someone else? What is desirable but optional?

As this at first looks like a chaos of decisions that you just can't get right, you might want to lay out a matrix to help you make those decisions. There is a lot of data worth collecting about a single object, but when you are laying out your strategy you should contemplate which data is crucial to fetch now and which might not be that important. There are in general four questions (each of which later might be a field in your database) to ask about every object data and with a few exceptions the answer is different for every project.

1. How important is this object data for distinguishing this object from similar objects in your own collection?
2. How important is this object data for the future work with the collection? Think small here, considering only the work you will have to do with the collection. If you widen the scope to future researchers, you will end up marking all the object data as highly important, which is true but not very helpful at this stage of the project.
3. How important is this object data for keeping the object safe? Think of issues like retrievability and doubtless identification, as well as climatic and legal aspects.
4. How important is the object data for future projects? Opposed to question number 2, this is about projects that will help you improve the collection, like storage planning or applying for grants.

Table 7.1 is a first matrix sample (as always, it's not exclusive):

Table 7.1.   Documentation strategy—generic sample

Object data	Importance for distinguishing objects from similar ones	Importance for future work with collection	Importance for object safety (physically, legally)	Importance for future projects (ie., storage planning, funds, crowdsourcing)
Accession number	high	high	high	high
Object name	high	high	low	high
Donor information	depends	depends	high	depends
Date of manufacturing	low	high	low	depends
Picture	high	depends	depends	depends
Measurements	depends	depends	depends	depends

The number of instances of "depends" in table 7.1 is deliberate and logical. This matrix has to be shaped to the specific situation you are dealing with. Let's do a few examples so you get the idea:

Example 1. A collection of about 5,000 radios. Your working contract runs only for a year, so you know you won't be able to catalog the whole collection in your tenure. There is a very active club of radio amateurs in your community that offered to volunteer in the process. You decided together with the board that you can't provide physical access to the collection for the volunteers, but you will provide some basic data in a database that is accessible online to the club members so they can do the detailed cataloging. Your matrix will probably look like table 7.2.

Example 2. A collection of farming equipment is stored under less than ideal conditions in an old equipment shed. City officials have offered three different places the collection could be moved to and asked you to decide which one would be the best and to provide a cost estimate for the needed storage furniture and packing materials, a time schedule for the move, and an estimate of how many staff members you need to relocate the whole collection. Your matrix will probably look similar to table 7.3.

As you see in these examples, your documentation strategy will look different every time, because the foundation for this type of strategy to be a success is to consider all circumstances that play a role in this process. It is also important to recognize that this method doesn't mean to define a certain set of object data fields you will fill in your database and totally ignore that there is other useful information contained in the objects that is worth being included. A "documentation strategy" is seldom one single step after which all information gathering is done, but more likely it is a set of steps where you first identify what needs to be captured immediately and define later

Table 7.2. Documentation strategy—example 1

Object data	Importance for distinguishing objects from similar ones	Importance for future work with collection	Importance for object safety (physically, legally)	Importance for volunteer-based cataloging project
Accession number	high	high	high	high

The accession number is crucial for any further work and reference.

Object name	high	high	low	low

As long as you make sure that the radios are properly photographed (including the manufacturing label), you can probably keep this pretty generic as the volunteers can extract the information from the pictures and add data like types, models, and manufacturers in the catalog.

Donor information	depends	depends	high	low

As the donor information can't be drawn directly from the objects, this should be included in the documentation. However, it is not important for the volunteer cataloging project, so it doesn't need to be and in fact shouldn't be included in the online database.

Date of manufacturing	low	high	low	low

Subject of research done by the volunteers, so nothing you need to research.

Picture	high	high	depends	high

The pictures are the basis of the volunteer project. As volunteers won't get access to the real objects, pictures have to contain all the details needed for volunteers' research, including manufacturing labels and, eventually, pictures taken with the backboard removed so volunteers can draw conclusions from the components used.

Measurements	low	depends	low	low

Radios are mass-produced objects and their measurements can be found in mailing catalogs and manufacturer's brochures. While there is a certain risk of inaccuracies, volunteers can use the measurements they've found in research.

circumstances under which you will add additional information. Be careful to define these "later circumstances," as they have the tendency of translating into "never" if not properly defined. In example 1 it is the moment the database is online and the proper data input is done by the volunteers (and preferably checked by a museum professional). In example 2 it is the time directly after the move. Preferably the order in which the objects will be examined after the move is already laid out in the documentation strategy.

To make this a little bit clearer, let's take a third example that is a very common one: you are the director of a small museum way back in the country and, as it often goes, you are the cashier, curator, janitor, educator, registrar,

Table 7.3.   Documentation strategy—example 2

Object data	Importance for distinguishing objects from similar ones	Importance for future work with collection	Importance for object safety (physically, legally)	Importance for storage move
Accession number	high	high	high	high

The accession number is crucial for any further work and reference.

| Object name | high | high | low | low |

You will need a name for each object, but as you have a tight schedule, there is no time for in-depth research. You will probably end up with the most generic term possible—eventually only a category name to go back to and do a more detailed cataloging after the move.

| Donor information | depends | depends | high | low |

As the donor information can't be drawn directly from the objects, it should be included in the documentation. On some occasions the donor information can be determined from the place and position an object is stored (i.e., all objects donated by Mr. Smith were stored in Room 3). In this case there is a risk of destroying this relationship during the move and it should be documented immediately. Otherwise, adding this information can wait until after the move.

| Date of manufacturing | low | high | low | low |

Subject of research that can be done after the move.

| Picture | high | high | depends | depends |

Having pictures of the whole collection would make sure that nothing is lost during the move and would help in setting insurance claims if you use a shipper for the move and something is damaged or lost. However, given your limited time, you might choose to take overview pictures of several objects together before they are packed into boxes.

| Measurements | depends | high | high | high |

The measurements are crucial for your planning process. They help you to determine what storage furniture and packing materials you will need, and the measurements of larger objects might guide your decision of choosing between the several offered storage places. For more details on storage planning and estimations, read chapter 8, "Storage Wants and Storage Needs."

marketing officer, and roofer—all in one person with no intern or volunteer in sight. Your predecessor has left you a decent amount of backlog in the collection, namely a small room not much larger than a broom closet with a variety of objects from a feathered headdress with a label reading "Original Headdress, probably Hopi," to an old oil can with the label of the local gas station.

To complicate matters, your predecessor was a passionate hoarder who believed that everything anybody brought to him somehow fit into the collection, making it impossible for you to decide if the oil can came in there for maintenance purposes or was actually accessioned as part of the collection. (One of the first things you did on the job was to establish a collections policy—the first one in the history of the museum.) To make matters worse, your predecessor had professional mood swings—one time he accessioned every single item in a toolbox, and another time he just gave one accession number to a whole tea service. Then there was the other time he didn't accession a single object for years, although he obviously accepted various donations.

Because you love bringing order into chaos, you decide to tackle the backlog every time you have a day or two without any other duties. Other than in the first two examples, there is some documentation, but what was said about the collection is also true about the files: for some objects you have a complete paper trail with deeds of gifts and additional correspondence, while others didn't even leave a mark in the ancient inventory book.

In a way, this situation is more complicated than a totally unmanaged collection: you can't just start accessioning the collection, you always have to check if an object was already accessioned and if there is some additional information available. Your first attempt was to take an object from the backlog and go through the ancient inventory book to see if you found an entry that resembled this object. If you were able to identify one without doubt, it got the old accession number; if you didn't find anything like it, you accessioned the object. You also created a place for the objects you weren't sure were the same as ones mentioned in the inventory book. Realizing that this takes a very long time and is very cumbersome, you switched to developing a documentation strategy that could look like table 7.4.

Table 7.4.   Documentation strategy—example 3

Step 1	• Take a picture of every object with a scale in front so one can roughly estimate dimensions.
	• If the object has an accession number attached, name the picture after that accession number. If it hasn't, attach a temporary number to the object and name the picture accordingly. (This is one of the rare occasions where a temporary number makes sense; we will discuss this later in this chapter.)
	• Record the following object data: accession or preliminary number, object name. Add things you find noteworthy, such as "remarks."
	• (Depending on your local settings, this can be done with pen and paper or by using a spreadsheet software. Pen and paper holds the advantage that you are not dependent on power supply and that your information will not be lost in case of a computer failure. The spreadsheet software holds the advantage

that you can search it for certain terms later and sort the list, thus you are able to compare certain objects. The safest way is to note the data with pen and paper and enter it into a spreadsheet software as soon as possible, keeping your original paper files for later reference to check writing errors. This takes a little longer, however, and holds the danger of transcription errors.)

Step 2
• Go through all the missing objects in the inventory book and search for those items on your spreadsheet (be creative in finding synonyms).
• Give every object you can identify without doubt its accession number and do a proper catalog entry in your database. "Proper catalog entry" means to complete the set of fields you deem necessary for cataloging objects and that is preferably in accordance with current "best practices" in museum documentation. Make a note in your excel spreadsheet about the transition.
• If you assume that an object is the one you've found in the inventory book but you aren't completely sure, just note the possible accession numbers in your spreadsheet. You won't create a database entry for it at the moment because while you work through the process, you might find another object to which the accession number belongs.
• After step 2 you have three object groups: accessioned objects, objects that might have been accessioned in the past, and objects with unknown acquisition status.

Step 3
• Do proper documentation by cataloging objects that might have been accessioned in the past. You give the object a new accession number but you indicate which old accession number it could be. Most database software has a special field for doing this reference. When you find proof that your assumption was right and the object is really the one accessioned years ago, you can link the new data set to the old accession number. If you find out the object was never accessioned you already have a valid new record.

Step 4
• Take a look at the remaining objects you couldn't find a match or probable match for in the inventory book. Separate them into those that fit into your mission and scope of collections and therefore should be accessioned and those that don't fit and therefore should find a new home.
• Accession those that fit into the collection and give them proper documentation.
• Find a good home for the other objects. Unlike properly accessioned objects, these objects don't require you necessarily follow the deaccession process, but as the objects probably made it into the collection because it was intended to hold them in public trust, you might want to apply the same due diligence in choosing a new home.

Step 5
• Go through the inventory book again and create a spreadsheet of all those objects you didn't find while working on the backlog. When you find new objects, it is easier to search this document than the inventory book.

Table 7.4 shows just one simple example for a documentation strategy. As you can see it starts with defining a set of data that is absolutely necessary for the comparing of the objects you find in the storage room with the objects noted in the inventory book. It keeps this amount of data to an absolute minimum, reducing the time it takes to go through the whole backlog. Having this minimum inventory in a spreadsheet and pictures of each object means you can do the next working steps at your desk, without having to access the storage room. You can compare a few pages of the inventory book with the spreadsheet whenever you have some time between other tasks. As you proceed you will be able to create new database entries for objects that were "lost" so far. You will also be able to create some space by deaccessioning objects that don't fit into the scope of your collections. At the end, there will be no more unknown objects in your museum—they will either have their old accession number or a new one, but they will have a number. Whenever an object "appears" in your museum you will be able to compare it with your inventory spreadsheet of missing objects and give it its original number, accession it anew, or find a new home for it.

Make sure you have a written record of your documentation strategy and keep a copy in your files so whoever has to deal with your collection in the future knows what you have decided to do and why. It is also a good idea to document the whole process so if you have to stop for some time you can easily find where you left off and proceed. For example, mark the shelves that are already photographed, mark (in a reversible way, of course) the entry you last checked in the inventory book, mark the object that has gotten a new database entry in your spreadsheet. Always remember: "be kind to your future self!"[4]

LAYING OUT A COLLECTIONS CARE STRATEGY

In some rare occasions you will be blessed with all the tools and archival packing materials you need to safely pack and store all the collections items you will process when executing your documentation strategy. And your storage conditions and individual working schedule allow you to create a custom-made storage box for every object you are working on. In this case, your collections care strategy is simple: you take an object, dust it or do whatever care treatment is necessary, document it, create a box, store it, take the next object, and so on.

However, it is more likely that your working environment looks like this: the storage conditions are poor, you don't have sufficient archival materials to store all the objects properly and taking the time to build a special box for

A REAL-WORLD EXAMPLE

Our motto for tackling the part of our collection that is in a poorly documented state is "En sak i taget," which more or less means "one thing after the other." We break it down into small, manageable tasks. For example, every Friday I take one closet of our textiles collection and go through its contents in the following way: I take an object out; search for the accession number; note the number or, if it doesn't have a number, note that there is none (entry : no number); and put it back in its place.

I take my notes and go back to my office. I check the numbers with the database (often to no avail). After this check I note the object in spreadsheet software so that I at least know the object's location. Working with the spreadsheet is faster than working with the database and I can import the spreadsheet into the database if necessary. Here's what I note in the spreadsheet:

- accession number
- object name (as close as possible; there are some things I just can't identify)
- location
- is there a database entry (yes/no)
- is there a picture in the database (yes/no)
- remarks (i.e., accession numbers that duplicate already existing accession numbers in the database, wrongly assigned pictures, information found on paper sheets in the vicinity of the object)

Objects that don't have an accession number attached get a "without number" in the field "accession number." Unfortunately there are many more of these. That way I get a good overview of how much there is still to accession and to photograph. On this basis, when projects are defined, it's easier to get funding to work on this backlog. Having some numbers at hand makes it easier to negotiate with upper management. Unfortunately my other duties don't allow me to do things like photographing or even dusting right then and there, but at least they are set to do later.

Susanne Nickel
Collections Manager
Eskilstuna Stadsmuseum
Eskilstuna, Sweden

a single object is time away from your documentation process and, worse, it means that a lot of other objects are in harm's way because of the poor storage conditions in the meantime. You still want to bring this collection into a best practice state in terms of packing and storing, but to reach this you need a more elaborate collections care strategy than the simple object-by-object strategy. Now, how do you do that?

Chances are that you've already sorted your collection with regard to the material the objects consist of and have spotted those objects that are especially delicate and in immediate need of treatment. Ideally you have already done something to improve the storage situation of those objects if you were able to. If not, you at least know which objects are top priority on your list. Need for collections care treatment may even vary within the same material group, so your strategy might involve immediate care for a certain object (i.e., a wedding dress that was crammed into a box) while putting other objects of the same group (i.e., a group of undergarments that are fairly acceptably stored right now even if the acidic box has to be replaced by an archival one in the future) on hold until later.

Laying out a collections care strategy, depending on your circumstances and your collection, is much more complicated than planning the documentation strategy. To make sure your decisions are reasonable and that all aspects are considered, make sure you educate yourself about all the material groups and object types you have in your collection. Make sure your information is up-to-date, because research in conservation is fast paced and what might have been considered "best practice" five years ago might now be totally outdated. Make sure you totally understand what harms a certain material group, why, and to what extent. This will help you prioritize and weigh risks against one another.

The problem with laying out a really good collections care strategy is that you have to make it generic enough to give you a general path to follow, while you also have to be aware that there is always a "depends." For example, you can define that all small objects should be dusted and then put into ziplock bags, but if you come across objects made out of celluloid, this would do more harm than good because those objects outgas components that will destroy the objects in the closed atmosphere of a bag. You can define that all household items should be vacuumed, but have to be aware that you shouldn't do this when they are varnished and the varnish is brittle. You can define that objects that contain problematic substances that have to be disposed of by a specialist are stored away from the other objects until you get funding to pay for the disposal, but if you come across a filled oil can that is rusty you have to take immediate action and let it be emptied by an expert right now. Some issues are foreseeable and can be covered by the strategy; others will only become apparent while working with the collection. A good collections care strategy tries to cover the standard cases but should also include warnings about when not to follow it.

As you see, the collections care strategy is dependent on the situation and collection, so it is impossible to establish a framework for it. But to give you an idea of what it might look like, let's take again the example 3 from earlier in this chapter. Looking at your supply of archival materials you realize that you only have a few archival boxes, a small amount of Ethafoam®, and two rolls of acid-free tissue paper left. Your tight budget is already stressed, so there is no chance of getting any new material until spring of next year. You heard the historical society in the neighboring city is about to order a large quantity of ziplock bags and they are willing to order some for you, too, so you can get them at the same reduced price they get for ordering in bulk. The local scout pack (you might remember them from chapter 6) launched a fund-raiser called "Begging for Bags" and collected enough money to buy you 200 ziplock bags of different sizes for smaller artifacts.

So, as you are tackling the backlog, what does your collections care strategy look like? Table 7.5 shows a sample collections care strategy.

As in the documentation strategy, the "later" needs to be defined or it will translate into "never." For example: you will inspect and separate the textiles; if you detect moth infestation you will bag your textiles and bring them to the historical society that has a freezer to treat them. When you bring them, you will talk with the society's expert for textile objects about the best way to store them. Whenever you have enough time and material, you will start building special mounts and boxes for them. You also apply for grants to buy special cabinets for them.

You get the idea that bringing your entire collection to overall "best practice" condition will take some time, but by following your strategy you will get a lot of objects in an acceptable state for long-term storage in a reasonable time.

INTERLINKING BOTH STRATEGIES

Note that the documentation strategy and the collections care strategy cannot be separated. Instead when you have laid out both, the next step is to interlink them. The steps have to be taken in a sequence that makes sense and is the most effective. For example, taking a picture of a dirty object and dusting it directly afterward is apparently the wrong sequence. It can be quite an effort to find what has to be done first and what should be done later, but without investing this effort you will certainly get confused in the working process.

Table 7.5. Collections care strategy

What objects?	What to do	When to do it
All objects	Check for health risks, pest infestation, mold, or other issues before proceeding. In case of doubt, call a specialist.	immediately
Household items, tools	Dust them with a soft brush and/or the vacuum cleaner. (Even if it is just a common household vacuum cleaner and a better one is on your material wish list, make sure it has a HEPA filter, otherwise you will just spread the dust)	immediately
Small objects	Put them in ziplock bags, if material allows.	immediately
Bigger objects	Put them in a box or cover them with clean sheets.	immediately
Drinking glasses, vases, ceramics, china	Put them aside in a safe way, maybe stored in a box that is marked "fragile" and is stored in a shelving unit with all the other fragile objects.	immediately
Drinking glasses, vases, ceramics, china	Build a special box for them.	later
Textile objects	Monitor for moth infestation or other pests.	immediately
Textile objects	Separate them from the rest of the collection, preferably into a room that is separated from the rest of the collection and the galleries.	immediately
Textile objects	If moth infestation detected, treat against moths.	later
Textile objects in general	Build special boxes or mount.	later
Extremely delicate textile objects, i.e., gowns and dresses	Build padded hangers, special boxes, or mounts.	immediately
Textile objects	Store in special cabinets.	later
Oil cans, rusty	Properly dispose of the content. (Disposal might have to be done by a specialist.)	immediately
Oil cans, not rusty	Properly dispose of the content. (Disposal might have to be done by a specialist.)	later

Taking example 3 again, we see in table 7.6 what your working process for most objects could look like. The letter in the last row indicates if it is a step from the documentation strategy (D) or the collections care strategy (C).

In larger collections or in collections with varied material groups, you might have to lay out different strategies for different material/object groups. As mentioned before, your strategies always list the standard approach, while you and everybody working with the collection have to be aware that there are exceptions to the rule. Some objects might be too fragile or damaged to

Table 7.6. Interlinked documentation/collections care strategy

Step 1	Check for pest infestation.	C
Step 2	Dust the object.	C
Step 3	Take picture of object.	D
Step 4	Attach number.	D
Step 5	Rename picture after number.	D
Step 6	Enter object data into spreadsheet.	D
Step 7	Pack object (either for long-term storage or temporarily for further processing like pest treatment or later box building).	C
Step 8	Compare spreadsheet to inventory book.	D
Step 9	Exchange preliminary number for real accession number when/if found.	D
Step 10	Do proper database entry.	D
Step 11	Treat for pests (if necessary).	C
Step 12	Build special box.	C
Step 13	Store in special cabinet (if necessary).	C

such an extent that dusting it yourself might cause additional damage. Those objects need another strategy and might have to be put aside until you can afford a specialized conservator. Some large and heavy objects like machines might require a specialist who tells you if and how you can move the object safely and how you should treat it.[5] Some collections might be so specialized that you have to bring in an expert to catalog them properly because you spent hours trying to identify what these objects are and yet you are still missing information to determine if they are important or not for the collection. In short: there is seldom a "one size fits all" strategy, and more likely you will have to lay out different strategies and define exceptions that, of course, should also be documented in your files.

While laying out your strategies, you might define some tasks or whole procedures that, because they are easily defined and can be done with little training and do not require much supervision, simply shout out for being assigned to an intern or volunteer. Mark them as such or create a special file so you have a record to refer to whenever you have a chance to get help. You might also define tasks and strategies that call for an expert. Whenever you think "it would be good if an archaeologist/conservator/engineer could do this," mark it as such; you never know when you might stumble upon such an expert who is willing to help.

One last word on strategy: Don't leave out steps that you find necessary but think will never be achieved. If you decide that some object needs to be treated by a specialized conservator or needs special storage requirements, define it as a step. Having it defined helps you to know that your collection is still not in the best possible condition and you have something at hand for those rare occasions where money for a certain measure is available.

THE ASSEMBLY LINE AND OTHER TRICKS OF THE TRADE

I can't remember who said it but I once heard, "There are no shortcuts in collections management." This is certainly true. If you miss getting a deed of gift signed, you will struggle to prove ownership later. If you accession objects without checking if they fit into your scope of collections, you have to deaccession later. If you neglect housekeeping in your collection, you have to fight pests later. If you don't document properly, you'll spend a lot of time searching for objects and information later. If you don't store properly, you have to pay conservation costs later. In almost all procedures in collections management if you skip a step in the beginning, it translates into much more time, effort, and expenses later.

Having said that, there are a few tricks for how to improve the workflow when working with your collection. They have nothing to do with skipping steps, but with organizing the working process in the most effective manner.

A good example is taking pictures of objects. If you include this in your documentation process and do it object by object, there will always be a time when you have to get up, adjust the light and position of the object in the best way, and take the picture. When you take a digital picture you have to save and rename it on your computer. When you take an analog picture you have to take down a note of what you've photographed to file the picture once the film is developed. However you do it, you will have to spend a considerable amount of time doing this step. It becomes a lot faster if you separate taking pictures from the rest of the documentation work. For example: you note the accession number and object name of ten objects, then you take them to your photographing space and take the pictures one after the other. It becomes even faster if you can possibly sort these objects by sizes, because you only have to adjust the camera and lights to this size and do a whole range of similar objects without changes.

If you photograph your objects, have all possible uses in mind. For documentation, you might like to include a scale so you can roughly estimate the dimensions later. But if you need a picture of the same object for a press release or an exhibition catalog, seeing the scale might not be preferable. To avoid having to take new pictures in the future, place the scale in a way so it can be easily cropped out with image software later—and make sure you photograph with a resolution that is suitable for printing.

Another trick for the time-consuming task of taking measurements: Here you have to change your position a couple of times: You take one dimension and either type it in the database or write it on paper; you take the next dimension. The absolutely best way to measure—because it is both safest and fastest—is to do it with another person. One person measures, the other person types or writes the measurement, saying it out loud to cross-check that it is correct. If there isn't the possibility of having a helper, you might consider how exact your measurements need to be. If an inch is close enough, you might skip individual measurement and add a scale—or better, a cube of scales—to your photographing space. That way the measurements can be drawn from the picture later. Consider doing this even if you need more exact measurements in the later documentation. You might get a rough idea of dimensions now and do a few days of "measurement activity" later, when you happen to have an intern or volunteer. Bernd Kießling, a colleague of mine, had to catalog a large collection of electronic tubes. He attached a tape measure to his worktable just in front of his keyboard. This allowed him to measure the tubes without having to take out the tape measure and he could type the measurements into the database while looking at it.

You might not be able to foresee the most effective working style before you start. Many things will become obvious while you are doing the actual work. Whenever a process seems to take up a lot of time, consider whether there's another way to organize it. As a rule of thumb, take a look at all the steps where you either change your own position or the position of the object. That's most likely where the workflow can be streamlined. Sometimes it doesn't even have to do with the object itself, but with movements you make. You might realize that having the printer on the other side of the table or adjusting your working table to a different height speeds up your working process considerably.

TEMPORARY NUMBER OR ACCESSION NUMBER?

One is easily tempted to give the whole collection temporary numbers at first and assign accession numbers later. However, I have seen this process gone wrong in so many different ways and on so many occasions that I strongly recommend immediately assigning valid accession numbers. At least once a week I stumble upon a temporary number dating from a documenting process done in the 1990s or early 2000s, and most of the time there isn't a list of which temporary number was transitioned into which accession number in the files, let alone do they appear in the database. The reason often stated for giving temporary numbers is that in the first step of documentation, you don't know if the object already has an accession number or, if it hasn't, if the object should remain in the collection or needs a new home. While this is true, temporary number create a whole range of issues:

- You have to write a list of which temporary numbers were transitioned into which accession numbers. As every list entry is done manually (no matter if typed or written) it increases the potential for errors, which creates a whole range of possibilities of assigning the wrong number to the wrong object. Matters get even more complicated when you rename pictures after temporary numbers only to rename them once again after accession numbers, and when you enter those picture numbers in your list of numbers. All the dealing with numbers is notorious for confusion and can be problematic.

• You have to attach first a temporary number to the object to replace it later with the "real" accession number. Although the temporary number will only be attached with a label while the accession number probably will be attached with a label and written on the object, it means you have to handle all the objects twice for mere numbering purposes. Not to mention that labels have a certain tendency to get lost, in which occasion you have to start all over again.

• You have an additional working step: At some point in the process you will have to change the temporary number into a "real" accession number once you are sure you want the object to be in your collection. Then, you have to make sure this renumbering is done everywhere the temporary number was used in the process, and you have to make sure that all of this is documented appropriately. The risk of forgetting something and not following through is very high.

Assigning a valid accession number right from the start holds a couple of advantages:

• If the object was never accessioned, it has a valid accession number right from the start that does not need to be changed later.

• If an older accession number is discovered at some point the new number can be cross-linked with the old number in the database and the data gathered under the new accession number can be imported into the documentation of the old, valid number. Of course you have to make sure that you follow through with changing the new number into the old and valid one everywhere you used the new one. But, unlike using a temporary number, it isn't that problematic if you missed changing it somewhere. You will always find the valid accession number by checking the database using the no-longer-valid accession number.

Having said that, there is a time and a place for a temporary number as you have seen in example 3. In a scenario where the number of items to process is limited, the number of objects that get a temporary number is even smaller and it is very likely that you are the person who supervises the process from the beginning to the end, so there is a chance that the temporary number won't really cause confusion. However, lay out the whole documentation strategy first and weigh the advantages of using a temporary number against an accession number carefully before you make your decision. And if you decide in favor of the temporary number, make sure you are documenting the whole process well enough so that replacing the temporary number with a valid accession number later is easy to do.

THE FOURTH LOGICAL EXIT AND YOUR OWN PATH

A collections manager's work is never done. There are always things one can do to improve the situation. You have reached the fourth logical exit when you have the following:

- a documentation strategy;
- a collections care strategy;
- a set of strategies that are interlinked documentation and collections care strategies for different object or material groups and eventually some tasks for interns or specialists that derive from these strategies.

From now on you define your own logical exits. As this is very individual to your collection, no book can help you any further. To give you an idea what future logical exists could look like, let's take a look at the examples 1–3 we used in this chapter:

Example 1, the radio collection that will be cataloged by volunteers:

Fifth logical exit: all objects numbered, photographed and uploaded to the online database, all object locations noted in a nonpublic version of the database.

Sixth logical exit: all object data researched and entered in the database by volunteers.

Seventh logical exit: all objects packed in archival materials.

Example 2, the collections move under time pressure:

Fifth logical exit: complete photographic overview of the current storage situation, a rough collections move strategy, and storage planning on basis of an overview of the collection, without detailed data.

Sixth logical exit: all objects numbered, named, and measured. (This could also be separate sequential logical exits if you process the whole collection in distinct categories.)

Seventh logical exit: detailed collections move plan, including a logistic concept, a list of needed packing materials and an estimate of needed staff diversified by skills (project manager, art handler, shipper, etc.).

Eighth logical exit: the move completed, all location changes documented.

Ninth logical exit: every object has a proper and detailed catalog entry. (Again, this could be sequential logical exits if you process the whole collection in distinct categories.)

Example 3, the backlog:

Fifth logical exit: all objects photographed, numbered, and named.

Sixth logical exit: a proper catalog entry for all objects you could identify as previously accessioned without doubt, a list of objects that might have been accessioned in the past, and a list of objects with unknown acquisition status.

Seventh logical exit: a proper catalog entry with a new accession number for all objects that might have been accessioned previously but couldn't be identified without doubt.

Eighth logical exit: a proper catalog entry with a new accession number for all remaining objects that fit into the mission; all objects that didn't fit into the mission are off to better homes; there is a list of missing objects that once were accessioned according to the old documentation.

Whatever your circumstances are, remember to break down all tasks into logical, manageable steps and to celebrate every logical exit you reach.

Now, let's take a closer look at our storage area.

NOTES

1. Alex Dawson and Susanna Hillhouse, eds., *SPECTRUM 4.0.* London: Collections Trust, 2011.

2. Daniel B. Reibel, *Registration Methods for the Small Museum*, Lanham, MD: AltaMira Press, 2008.

3. In the following, I use "documentation" for the overarching process of object documentation that contains the accessioning of an object, its cataloging, establishing references to other objects in the collection, and the research and filing of any documents that comes with that process, like "deeds of gift" or user's manuals. I use "accessioning" for the process of making an object part of the collection—that is, clearing the legal status and assigning an accession number. I use "cataloging" for the process of making the data of an object—whether handwritten on catalog cards or digital in a database—available for further use. This information contains both

intrinsic data like measurements, weight, color, and so forth, and extrinsic data like the donor or past use of the object.

4. Tracey Berg-Fulton, in her presentation "We Were Promised Jetpacks: What Does the Future Hold for Registrars?" on June 10 at the European Registrars Conference 2013 in Helsinki.

5. A common danger with machines is that most people tend to think that they are very sturdy, stable, and not easy to damage. The exact opposite is true. If you take a printing machine as an example: Those machines were built to be installed and secured to the ground. They were never meant to sit on pallets. If you move them, there is a high danger that they will tip over. If they have not been properly secured, some components can suddenly move, making the center of gravity shift and letting the machine topple over. Being made of cast iron, minor shocks or twists might cause breaks in machine parts that can't be restored. Each machine has its special risks and vulnerabilities and some of them contain health hazards like toxic hydraulic oil, so you should definitely consult a specialist before doing anything with machines.

Chapter Eight

Storage Wants and Storage Needs

It's very telling that whenever I start typing "storage" I want to add "issues" and meeting fellow collections managers often includes a game of "who's got the worst storage situation?" Somehow, even the colleagues from large museums with elaborate heating, ventilation, and air condition systems (HVAC) and compact storage have their wants and longings when it comes to storage. In an unmanaged collection you are far from moaning that you could really use more of those pullout storage panels for your paintings, you are dealing with much more basic issues. Luckily, there are a lot of programs and much literature out there that can help you assess and improve your storage—to name but a few, "Stewardship of Collections" module of the StEPs program (Standards and Excellence Program for History Organizations) by the AASLH, the ReOrg program supported by the UNESCO and ICCROM (http://www.re-org.info/), or the *Benchmarks for Collections Care* by the Museums Archives and Libraries Council in London.[1]

For a start, I would recommend that you read chapter 7 of part 1 of the *National Park Services Museum Handbook*[2] and chapter 1 of *Stewardship: Collections and Historic Preservation.*[3] Reading these, you will see that you have already applied some of the recommendations that are necessary for good collections care—for example, that you threw everything that isn't a collections item out of your storage area and that you've set up a working space. In other regards you see that you are still stuck deep down in the basics; you will probably have objects that are piled up and your climate is probably not as stable as you wish it were.

As so often has been the case during your working process, you know that you have to improve the situation and you have helpful literature, but the difficulties are how and where to start and how to proceed afterward. As Scott Carrlee so wisely says, "Collections Care is a continuum: Inside is better than outside; on a shelf is better than on the floor; in an enclosure is better than out in the open. A museum can always improve, no matter where it is on the continuum."[4] So, you just have to start off and improve gradually. But just as with documentation, you will need a strategy to do that. The good news is that you already have hit the ground running if you think of storage not in terms of a room or building, but as "successive layers of protective envelopes or enclosures, from the building itself to the equipment and containers that surround an object."[5]

You have already started improving storage from both sides a while ago. In chapter 4, where you were getting organized, you already started improving the largest of the protective envelopes, the building or storage room by using "Grandmother's Fixes." In the last chapter, when you laid out a preservation strategy for your objects, you thought about the smallest envelopes—the wrapping and housing for the single object—and you already gave some thought to the storage furniture you will need. On the basis of this groundwork it shouldn't be too hard to lay out a storage improvement strategy.

Note: I have skipped objects such as archival material, paintings, graphics and photographs, as well as textiles because there is indeed a considerable amount of literature dealing with how to store this material. Besides, this chapter would become too long and I would certainly only repeat something that is already written by a more experienced collections professional. Instead, I will concentrate on three-dimensional objects that aren't textiles. Those objects where the chapter on "Preventive Care" in MRM5 leaves you with the remark, "Three-dimensional objects present unique challenges that have to be resolved by creative staff members."[6] You may have already guessed it: the "creative staff member" is you!

A VISION OF SPACE

In all the previous chapters you have dealt with the circumstances you've found and worked toward improving the situation while accepting the realities. Apart from the best practice you've read about in the literature, and maybe your own ideal conception in your head, you didn't develop a vision of how your collection will look like when it's fully managed. But, in order to set up a strategy for continuously improving your storage conditions, you have to do exactly that: for one logical moment you have to act as if there were no hindering circumstances, as if there were no objects in your storage area and you had all the money in the world. Granted, it's easier to do if you will get a whole new storage area, but let's face it: this dream only comes true for very few of us. More likely you will have to live with the storage area you already have.

But what good is it to envision something that may never become reality? Well, here are several reasons why you need to:

1. Having a plan of how it could look in the future means having a vision of how things might change to the positive. When discussing refurbishing with upper management or potential financial supporters, you will be much more convincing having a vision and a master plan than just presenting a list of furniture you want to buy. In addition, it's of course much easier to pull a list of needed furniture, time needed to refurbish the storage, and estimated costs out of a master plan than out of the blue.
2. Having a plan of how a completely refurbished storage space should look makes it easier to break the process into smaller and easier to reach steps. If you have a certain budget to spend on furniture each year, you can decide when to buy what furniture and in which year you will have put the master plan into effect. If you don't have a certain budget but apply for grants, you can mark the plan with priorities, deciding what furniture has to be bought first and what can wait until later.
3. You avoid blocking yourself and your own work with *ad hoc* decisions on where to place new storage furniture. To make it a little clearer with an example, if you get the money to buy two new shelving units, you might feel tempted to set them up in a place that you have already cleared. As you continue working on your collection and clearing new space you might discover that the place where you set up the shelving units is now completely inconvenient. The shelves might block a certain wall where you want to install a collection of billboard signs, or they might be too close to the next wall to set up another shelving unit. If you have a master plan you can set those shelving units up where they belong in the long run.

DEVELOPING YOUR MASTER PLAN

In chapter 4 you created a plan of the situation as it is. Now, you take the same plan, but remove all the things that can be removed, so you have just your storage space. Time to start planning. But obviously, you can't just take a couple of storage furniture catalogs and draw in some furniture. You first need to give some thought to what to store and where to place it.

Step 1: Your Objects

It's a good thing you've sorted your objects because now you know them personally. Certainly, you are not through with documenting when you start planning your storage, but you have an idea of what you have. Some guidelines recommend that you have measurements of all your objects before you start planning your storage. This sounds logical and indeed might be the best situation, but in most cases it just isn't realistic. Instead, it puts the improvement of your storage off to a time that might never come.

But how can you plan storage without having exact object dimensions? You can't plan it in an exact way but there is one thing that comes in handy: most objects you have in history collections are objects that were used in everyday life, and, as they had to be handled by humans, few exceed the size and weight a human can carry around. Their sizes fall into certain categories and methods of storing. For a start:

1. Category XS—Really small objects: These objects, such as pins, gramophone needles, or coins, are often plentiful and still don't use up much space. You will have to keep them in larger containers so they won't get lost. For storage furniture, cabinets or open shelving is possible.
2. Category S—Small objects: These are objects you carry around every day to perform certain tasks by using them with your hands. This category contains "tools" in the widest sense of the word like spoons, knives, scoops, wrenches, hammers, knitting needles, and other devices of everyday use such as cups, plates, bottles, cameras. Small as they are they usually can be packed together with similar objects into boxes about the size of a shoebox. These boxes can also go in cabinets or on open shelving.
3. Category M—Mid-sized objects: These are objects you would normally carry around with two hands and, while larger than the objects of category S, still will not exceed the range of your arms. This is a very broad category and you will find objects as diverse as pots, typewriters, and scales in it. Some of them will fit in boxes; some might be stored only with a large Polyethylene (PE) or Tyvek® bag to protect them from dust. They might still fit into cabinets, otherwise open shelving is the way to go.
4. Category L—Large objects: These are objects that are larger than those described in category M. While there might be some you can still carry around without help, such as chairs, ladders, or paddles, most will exceed either the weight or the size you can carry alone, such as TV sets, plows, or baking ovens. Because they exceed the size of boxes they might be stored in larger open shelving or on pallets on the floor or in heavy duty racks so they can be handled with special equipment.
5. Category XL—Really large objects: Here we leave the sizes that can be carried around by humans. These are machines, vehicles, and larger furniture. You will need some special equipment (at least dollies) to handle them and most of the time the floor is the place they are stored, wherever possible elevated off the ground by pallets or other devices so they are safe in case of a water leak.

Step 2: Estimating Your Space Requirements

You should be able to roughly estimate how many objects of the different size categories you have. To plan your needed storage furniture you might need to get a little more precise.

For XS and S objects you can use the available standard sizes of archival boxes as a measurement: pack a few of these boxes (or other boxes that are roughly this size) and try to determine how many objects fit in them safely. You need to pack a few sample boxes to get an average of objects that comfortably fit. If you have done that, you can count or estimate the number of objects that you have in this size category and divide them by the number of objects you've found fit into a box. This will give you an idea of how many boxes you need.

Then you have to find out how many boxes fit into your preferred storage furniture. You can get the measurements of cabinets, shelving units, drawers, and shelves from vendors. Also make sure you research the maximum weight those devices can support. If you plan to stack some boxes on the shelves, make sure the boxes can be stacked safely and find out how much weight the boxes can support, as the box below has to carry the weight of all boxes stacked above it. Stacking boxes can save space but experience shows that stacking more than two boxes is seldom a good solution, even if they support the weight in theory. The danger comes from handling those boxes: The total weight of a stack of boxes is often underestimated, so the person removing the stack of boxes from the shelf realizes too late that they are too heavy for him or her to carry and lets the boxes drop. On other occasions people try to pull out the box from below, making the boxes above crash on the shelf or—worse—on the floor. In most cases it's safer and more practical to add an additional shelf instead of stacking boxes.

It's easier to estimate for category M objects that fit into boxes because normally not more than one object fits into a box, so you just have to figure out how many of these boxes fit into your preferred furniture. For objects that don't fit into boxes (or that you prefer not to have in boxes) you have to find out how many of these objects fit on a shelf of your preferred furniture. It might help here to refine the size category to allow you to get more precise. It helps to create a set of imaginary boxes that the objects fit into. While you won't have boxes in these sizes, they help you to define in which size category an object fits. The higher the similarity of the size, the more accurate your estimate gets. This might lead to interesting discoveries, that toasters have roughly the same space requirement as handbags and portable radios, as do coffee makers, juicers and microscopes and flower pots, professional flour sieves and transceivers. As you can guess from this listing, storing in size categories might be the best for exact space estimation, but it soon reaches the point where it is all but practical.

On the positive side, no one (except maybe yourself) forces you to store with a focus on size categories only, for this is only a tool for your storage planning and space estimates. A 46-inch shelf might be too small to hold two considerably large radios from the 1950s, but might easily hold one of those radios and three portable radios. Here we are on the crossroads of estimation: You can either take objects of similar size, find out how many fit on one shelf, and calculate the number of shelves you will need for all the objects of this size. Or you can fill some experimental shelves with what seems to you as a good variety of objects you have of a certain kind and then divide the number of all the like objects by the average number of objects on one shelf and get the total number of shelves. Both methods will give you a good estimate; a more precise one can only be derived from measurements.

Be careful not to shoot yourself in the foot when packing your test shelves! To handle objects safely they need a little wiggle room around them to ensure that the collections are safely accessible. You can store one object in front of another if you provide the possibility to remove both and put the first one back after the removal of the second. If you don't have space for this (or can provide it temporarily by having a table trolley for handling objects) avoid storing two objects deep. It should go without saying that you must not stack objects. It's hard to determine how much handling space is actually needed around objects as it often depends on the measurements and weight of the objects, but we usually take about 5 inches or the thickness of a male arm as a rule of thumb for objects of the category M.

The larger the objects get, the more important the measurements become. The category L objects are in my experience still good to estimate. You can easily tell that two television sets fit on a standard pallets or that you can probably store four chairs on a 47-square-inch shelf. I try to find standard solutions in storage as much as possible for reasons I will mention later in this chapter. But as this size category is responsible for taking a lot of space, you should determine what goes where exactly, not as an estimate. Here, whether you have four or five TV sets makes the difference between whether you need two or three pallet spaces. Having more category L objects can add up to making the decision about whether you need two or three heavy duty racks, which is a significant difference both in space and money.

In category XL, estimations won't help you anymore. You will have to take the exact measurements and have to think carefully about where to store those objects.

Figure 8.1. Storage of the collection of varied household objects in a former storage hall of the Landesmuseum für Technik und Arbeit in spring 2006, TECHNOSEUM, Foto Angela Kipp

Figure 8.2. The same collection depicted in 8.1 stored in the new storage area of the TECHNOSEUM, March 2015, TECHNOSEUM, Foto Hans Bleh

A REAL-WORLD EXAMPLE

How do I know these rough estimations actually work? A while ago a colleague from a small historical museum brought up the issue and asked me how to estimate storage space. She said she might have the chance to get some storage furniture for her collection, but had to write a proposal fast, within a few weeks, before the end of the financial year. She had already researched resources on storage planning and contacted other colleagues, but admitted, "If you don't have your collection fully cataloged, measurements and all, it seems that there is no way to do it."

I thought about it and had to admit that I had so far made estimates only in two ways: either I had the measurements, or rough measurements, so I could make an educated guess, or I had to equip a blank storage space with as much furniture as possible, sometimes developing different scenarios showing different possibilities of price ranges and capacity. But it bothered me that I couldn't be of more help. Then it occurred to me that I actually had the tools to help. At the TECHNO-SEUM we have an area of about 600 square meters (6,458 square feet) that is equipped with 424 open, metal, shelving units, about 2 meters (6.56 feet) high with the shelves measuring 120 centimeters by 40 centimeters (47.24 by 15.75 inches) in varied heights, but usually having four shelves in one shelving unit. Stored there is virtually everything the collection of a small historical society holds with regard to very small to midsized objects—only more so. Where the small museum might have five coffee makers we have 350, instead of one razor we have thirty, instead of fifteen beer mugs we have 130—you get the picture, it's a historical collection on steroids. Over the years between 2006 and 2013 we improved storage conditions there, packing objects in better boxes, adding more shelves, and trying to find compromises between saving space and having similar object groups together. In 2015 we were close to reaching the maximum packing density there. Almost all of the 25,000 objects are well-documented so in the spirit of backward engineering I wondered if I could draw some helpful figures out of the database, applying a little bit of high school math.

I drew the number of objects from the first shelving unit and multiplied it by the number of shelving units I had in that row. Then I compared it to the number of objects that were actually in there. I did the same with all twenty-three rows of shelving units. What did the figures show?

There were rows where the estimate was very accurate, ranging from 0 percent to 10 percent off the estimation. But there were also rows where the estimate was over 100 percent off. What may come as a surprise was that the estimates of the rows that held a variety of household goods from large pots to tiny spoons were more accurate than the estimates for the rows that seemed to hold a more homogenous group of objects like radios or typewriters. I examined what made estimates inaccurate and found that it often derived from the way we stored like objects and how we often added small objects that were topically related to bigger objects (for example gramophone needles in the row where gramophones are stored) in the first shelving units of a row or side by side with bigger objects to save space (for example boxes with tapes beside the tape recorder they were accessioned with). Then, there were also shelving units that held close to zero objects because something was on loan or out for conservation. When I eliminated the disruptive factors by taking shelving units from the middle of a row—I randomly chose the fifth and later repeated the operation by taking five random shelving units out of a row—instead of the first, not counting shelves with zero objects and taking shelving with similar packing density as the basis of my calculations the figures became much more accurate, ranging between 0 percent and 10 percent off and most of the time the number of objects stored in there in reality was higher than the estimate.

Step 3: What Furniture Do You Need?

Now that you know how much space you will need, it's time to decide what this means in furniture. When you estimated the space requirements of your different size groups you already developed some rough ideas about storage furniture. For example you decided how deep and wide your shelves should be and how many different sizes of shelves would be required. This automatically leads to the different sizes of shelving units and cabinets you will need. With your objects in mind, you also know which definitely need to be stored in closed cabinets and for which open shelving units are acceptable. This should now give you an idea of what furniture you will need.

You will find a whole range of possibilities from really expensive solutions to cheaper ones from your local hardware store. Educate yourself about possible dangers cheaper solutions impose on your objects and be sure not to fall for seemingly cheap offers that draw unforeseen consequences. For example, wooden shelves may be cheaper than metal ones but have to be coated against off-gassing and may not be as strong. Cheap metal shelving units might be coated with off-gassing lacquer, have rough edges that cause injuries when setting them up, or might be made of less dense metal, which might lead to buckling of shelves when packed with too much weight. Often cheaper shelving units are not as easy to set up and changing the position of the shelves later can require quite an effort, not to mention that some have the tendency to lean because the construction of parts is inadequate for use. Sometimes shelving units are cheaper because the manufacturer discontinued this model, which means that you can't order additional shelves later. Before deciding on one type of shelving unit, use the "Power of Coffee" and talk to colleagues who already use them.

If you can already see from your figures that your space requirements exceed your actual storage space you should look into compact shelving. Whenever possible you should try to strive toward this solution because it saves so much space and often even allows for some reasonable growth in your collection so the initial investment pays off in the long run.

Depending on your location you will have to consider some common natural catastrophes in your area. Flood zones and earthquakes play a role in your master plan. Your shelving units might require protection against objects falling from the shelves and the units might have to be specially secured to the ground. The lower posts might require special protection against water and you might start with placing the first shelf higher above the ground than normal. It's always a good idea to use shelves that are strong enough to support the weight of the objects when they are wet. Make sure you have considered all the security measures and calculated their price.

When deciding on your storage furniture, don't forget to calculate what you need for your documents, paintings, graphics, photographs, and textiles, although I didn't mention them in the calculation above. Textiles might need specialized solutions with moth-proof cabinets and specialized deep drawers.

Step 4: How Do You Use Your Storage?

Now that you have calculated how much space you will need and what furniture you prefer you can start thinking about how to set this furniture up in your storage. This is where it is crucial to think about how you use your storage.

There is active and not-so-active storage. I shy away from calling a storage area "inactive," because it does create the wrong impression that nothing happens in there. I prefer to call the opposite of an active storage a "sleeping" storage. Sleeping storage is only accessed regularly for climate control, a checkup on the sticky traps, and some housekeeping. The occasions when it "wakes up" because some objects are removed for exhibitions, loans, or other purposes are rather few—maybe about once a month. The contrary is the "active" storage area. It is accessed a couple of times a week, sometimes even numerous times a day, to take out or bring in some objects for exhibition, documentation, or research. On which part of the spectrum your storage is determines how you can set up your storage furniture. A "sleeping" storage doesn't require a sophisticated logistical concept. You can set up the shelving units in a way the space is used best and it doesn't matter if it takes some time to take a certain object out. In an "active" storage you have to think about how to set up your furniture so objects can be handled quickly and safely.

For example, in a "sleeping" storage you can have objects stored two objects deep, take out the first, carry it to a table by the door, take the second object out, carry it to the table, and put the first object back on its place on the shelf. In an "active" storage you still can store the objects that way, but you will need a table trolley to make the exchange and therefore your aisle has to be broad enough to allow access for that trolley.

The "sleeping" and "active" mode might also apply to certain object groups. For example, if your museum contributes to a little toy exhibition at your local mall every year the toy collection should be stored in a more accessible manner than other parts of the collection.

For planning the layout of your storage furniture, think about what typical human-object interactions look like. How are objects removed? Where do they go from storage? What is done? How do they come back? You might discover that while you can set up more shelving units in long rows it might be better for the working process to have fewer shelving units in shorter rows—or vice versa. General recommendations might not be applicable to your individual setup. For example, you might prefer to have no furniture in the vicinity of the windows because you know that they are unreliable and you have often dealt with water issues in the past.

When you have considered your working processes and all other circumstances that are important for your storage, you should be able to draw a map of the furniture in your future storage.

Step 5: Draw Your Master Plan

It can be a challenge to make all the furniture you need fit into the storage room you have. You might try different layouts, switch between different possibilities of furniture, and even sometimes decide upon other storing methods for objects. I have done it numerous times and talked with a lot of other colleagues who had to do it and there seems to be no better solution than to just sit there and work through the available possibilities. Some colleagues prefer to do it with a software like Adobe Illustrator or Google SketchUp, others use graph paper and cut out scale furniture. I have even heard that full-size, cardboard mock-ups can be quite helpful. But all sit there in quiet and try to make it fit. So you know what you will have to do in this step.

Clearly, all aisles should be broad enough for safe handling of the objects and you should follow every safety regulation for storage rooms. That you must leave important appliances such as power outlets, light switches, switch boxes, windows, and doors free of furniture, is also logical. Consider that working equipment like table trolleys and tables need to have a defined space in your map, for they are easily forgotten and block the way later.

If you have XL objects it's often easiest to define where they will have their place and work from this size category down. Always consider how the objects can be taken out of the room. If you have a 1950s Chevrolet in your collection, you condemn it to a life behind the scenes when you block its way to the entrance gate with heavy-duty racks. This example is only slightly exaggerated, blocking the way out for objects is a common danger.

When drawing up your plan you might discover different possible solutions. This can be a great starting point for developing storage improvement and actually points far beyond that. For example, you discover how many objects you could store in compact shelving versus conventional open shelving. Drawing both possibilities, you can list prices, objects stored, and space for collection development in percentage growth per year. Make sure your plans and figures are well founded because this is a great starting point for discussing funding for storage furniture and other issues with upper management.

Step 6: Good Furniture Is Not Enough

Until this stage you have concentrated on the furniture. But right from the start, when you first met your collection in chapter 2, you realized a lot of things that needed improvement. Some burning issues you fixed with "Grandmother's Fixes" in chapter 4, but you need more professional solutions in the long run.

Now is the time to list those issues and present possible solutions. A better insulation of the outside walls, better windows, an HVAC system or at least more reliable heating—all this should be laid out in your master plan. Research what should be done and how much it will cost.

It's the same with tools and archival materials you need to get your work done. Write down an estimate of what you need and how much it will cost.

Make sure that for now and a considerable time forward, you have written down everything you need. Don't forget costs for renting specialized equipment like a forklift or a crane for moving heavy objects and costs for experts like conservators if needed. If your master plan involves a working process for which you will need additional helpers, add an estimate on needed man-hours and needed specialization.

Step 7: Presenting Your Master Plan

If you are not the single decision maker in your institution (and chances are you aren't), you will have to present your master plan to upper management to get it funded. But even if you are free to choose what to do and when, you will probably need to apply for funds or convince donors to help you with funding your plan.

In any case, make sure your figures are as accurate as possible. No one likes to give money for a project only to have the same person ask later for more money for the same project. You can present different scenarios with different costs, pointing out advantages and disadvantages—for example the pros and cons of using customized versus standardized packaging, or using in-house staff versus external staff for setting up shelving units.

When presenting to upper management, think about what figures you can present in addition to the obvious better long-term collections care—for example a more space-saving storage method translates into cost saving in heating, electricity, and rent for an additional storage room. You can relate the percentage of yearly growth of the collection with the space that is still free in the different storage solutions and convert it into years until additional storage is needed. This will give upper management an idea as to how fast new storage will be needed in both scenarios and if the accessioning strategy of the following years can be active or should be very cautious.

MAKING YOUR VISION COME TRUE

If your master plan is fully approved and funded by upper management, you probably should play the lottery because this seldom happens. More likely you get parts of it approved or you are granted a smaller portion of the budget than needed.

Now you have to break your master plan down into doable next steps. As you did in your documentation strategy, take a look at the objects in the most urgent need of good storage furniture. Chances are they are the most delicate objects, but that's not inevitably so. It might be that you decide for some larger, open shelving to get the kitchen chairs and bedside tables off the floor to gain more moving space for the work on the smaller objects.

Table 8.1 shows an example of how a storage improvement strategy, on the basis of a master plan, could look, including estimated date for completion:

As you see in this table, as soon as you got funding for a certain project or furniture (in this case assumed to arrive in January), you take the next step in your master plan, using the time until the next funding arrives to fill the furniture and to improve other aspects of collections care. Of course, your storage

Table 8.1. Example schedule tight budget

Step 1	Buy and set up 2 heavy duty racks with 24 pallets for farming machinery and tools.	March Year 1
Step 2	Pack and store farming machinery and tools in the racks.	April–May Year 1
Step 3	Sort and document textiles and small tools; see documentation strategy for detailed sequence.	June–October Year 1
Step 4	Prepare for window exchange: Remove all objects from the wall with the windows, protect rest of collection so it doesn't get harmed during the work.[1]	November–December Year 1
Step 5	Replace old windows with new ones. Put back removed furniture and objects.	January–March Year 2
Step 6	Continue sorting and documenting textiles and small tools; see documentation strategy for detailed sequence.	April–December Year 2
Step 7	Buy specialized textile cabinets and store the textile collection in them.	January–March Year 3
Step 8	Continue documenting small tools and household equipment; see documentation strategy for detailed sequence.	April–December Year 3
Step 9	Buy and set up metal shelving for small objects rows A–C; buy archival boxes for small objects.	January–February Year 4
Step 10	Repack small tools and store them in row A.	March–July Year 4
Step 11	Repack household equipment objects and store them in rows B–C.	August–December Year 4
Step 12	Buy and set up metal shelving for small to midsize objects and store them in rows D–E.	January Year 5
Step 13	Wrap furniture and store it in row D.	February–March Year 5
Step 14	Wrap or pack midsize farming tools and store them in row E.	April–June Year 5

1. Keep in mind that exchanging windows is a critical task when it comes to climate and security. In this scenario it is scheduled in winter—not only because funding comes at the beginning of each year, but also because it is assumed that there are some weather periods with cold but rather dry weather, so the heated storage area doesn't suffer an increase in humidity while the windows are replaced. This increase in humidity would certainly be the risk if you do exchange windows in spring, when the outside temperature is higher than inside the storage and it's wet outside. But this is very much dependent on your region, so make sure you've checked the weather dates from former years to get a feeling for when the best period for window exchange would be. And don't be afraid to change your schedule when you realize it doesn't work the way you've planned.

improvement strategy has to be interlinked with your documentation and collections care strategy. With your storage improvement strategy in place, your procedure is complete for tackling this collection, so from now on you "just" have to follow through.

But before I end this chapter, let's take a look at three special aspects of storage that should be given a further thought: the question of whether to use standard equipment versus customized, how to number storage furniture, and some common mistakes made while storing.

CUSTOMIZED VERSUS STANDARDIZED

During the experimentation phase, when trying to develop a good estimate on storage requirements, you might discover that you need different sizes of archival boxes for your objects. Some of the small objects might fit with similar objects in archival boxes that are roughly the size of a shoe box, some need to be longer, some flatter, some higher, and some might need a more square outline. When defining those sizes you might feel that it's better to build customized boxes for all those different sizes rather than trying to define what you need. If you have enough manpower you can certainly do that. If you haven't, you should consider choosing standardized boxes even if that means that you have to choose a box bigger than is absolutely necessary for an object.

Standardized archival boxes come in a variety of sizes and can be assembled quickly. Most of them are stackable and the standard size makes it easy to estimate their space need. Most of the standard-sized boxes fill standard-sized shelves quite well. With intelligent packing of a group of small objects inside the box you can use the provided space effectively. Concentrating on only a few standard sizes means that you can order larger quantities of the same size, which normally leads to price reduction. You will find standard sizes cover a wide range of object sizes; only a few will really need a customized form of packaging. Don't get me wrong: custom built boxes are awesome and in some cases are space savers, but be very careful to calculate the time and material you invest versus the advantage it brings.

It's the same with shelving units: While there is a time and a place for special solutions built by a specialist, most of the time standard solutions can be customized to the needed purpose. It pays to spend some time researching storage solutions both in- and outside of the museum world. Most of the time someone has already found a storage solution for your special storage issue.

LOCATION NUMBERING ISSUES

Your master plan is a great way to number your storage furniture consistently right from the start. For many storage areas, a common issue that grows over time is the issue of location numbering; it generally is not done consistently, which leaves you with a confusing location layout.

For example (take a look at graph 8.1 to follow this sequence): at the start of a collections improvement project there were ten shelving units in the middle of the room that got marked with the letter S (indicating that you are looking for a shelving unit; cabinets might have a C before their number) and numbers 1–10 (white). When an additional ten shelving units were funded, seven of them fit on the left-hand wall in a row and were marked S 11–17 (light grey). The remaining three shelving units were set up on the opposite wall, numbered S 18–20 (light grey). Unfortunately, there was no way to clear more space on this wall at that time. The next ten shelving units that were granted were set up as a row in the middle of the room, numbered S 21–30 (grey). Now, with this new space it was finally possible to clear space at the right hand wall, so the row S 18–20 was continued with the shelving units S 31–34 (dark grey). Someone who isn't familiar with the history of this particular setup of shelving units will have difficulties understanding it, not to mention finding anything.

You can avoid this kind of confusion if you plan your storage furniture ahead, for example, in a master plan as described earlier in this chapter. And you can make your life a lot easier if you switch to numbering your storage furniture differently.

In most cases it is preferable to combine the power of letters and numbers. Our alphabet is limited in characters but our numbers are endless. You can give rows of shelving units a distinct letter and then a sequence of numbers, so the first shelving unit is A 01 and the last shelving unit in the row is A 07. That way, whenever you get the next shelving units funded you can continue your setup without numbering issues. See graph 8.2 for the same setup numbered that way.

In bigger storage units like industrial halls, you might want to repeat the number of your chessboard grid as described in chapter 4, "Getting Organized," and then work with numbers or letters and numbers for your shelving units. This helps finding small shelving units in a huge area quicker. Here, your first shelving unit might be called "A 1 (the grid number) S A 01." See graph 8.3 for the same setup numbered with additional grid numbers.

As you see, this is a setup designed for larger storage areas. In smaller storage areas, like a single room, the grid numbers don't hold much advantage over simple lettered and numbered rows.

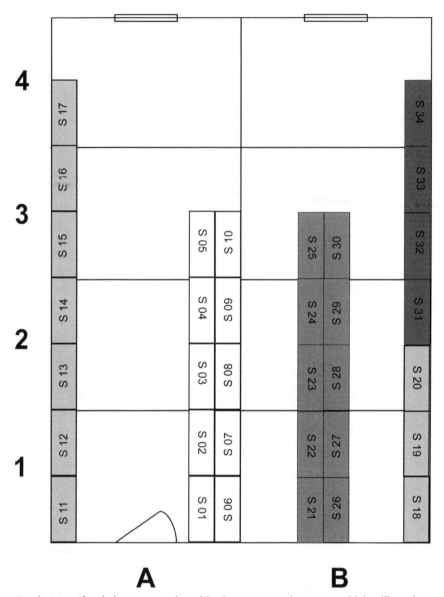

4
S 17

3
S 16
S 15

2
S 14
S 13

1
S 12
S 11

S 05   S 10
S 04   S 09
S 03   S 08
S 02   S 07
S 01   S 06

S 25   S 30
S 24   S 29
S 23   S 28
S 22   S 27
S 21   S 26

S 34
S 33
S 32
S 31
S 20
S 19
S 18

A   **B**

Graph 8.1.   The shelves are numbered in the sequence they came which will confuse future users.

A REAL-WORLD EXAMPLE

We were setting up a couple of heavy-duty storage racks for the temporary storage of an incoming collection of more than 100 TV sets at the
TECHNOSEUM. Assuming that we would get some more racks, we
numbered them in consistency with the racks that were already there,
leaving those numbers out we expected to come later. When the additional racks arrived that came from a separate storage area, we realized
that they weren't exactly the same size and therefore didn't fit. That's
why some of our rows now begin for example with "B 3," instead of
"B 1." In a similar setting we had to disassemble two shelving units to
get more moving space. That's why this row ends suddenly at "S 13"
and continues with "S 16." Because they are so illogical, storage in both
locations needs to be explained to new staff members.

Whenever confronted with the question of location numbering, you will
be confronted with the question of how detailed you should get. Should you
number individual shelves and exact positions on them? That's not an easy
question to answer because much will depend on how your storage is used.
In general, the more precise your location numbering is, the easier it is to retrieve objects. On the other hand, the more precise it is, the higher the danger
of putting an object back in the wrong place, noting the wrong location or
forgetting to note the location change at all. To make your decision, take a
look at what you noted in Step 4 of your master plan. The more your storage
use resembles a "sleeping" storage the more precise you can and should be in
location numbering; the more "active," the more you should strive toward a
system that forgives minor human errors.

At the TECHNOSEUM we have both. In the more "active" parts we only
number the shelving units, not the shelves, which provides us with the possibility of rearranging objects on different shelves as long as we keep this
object movement "vertically," which means within a certain shelving unit.
"Horizontal" object moves between shelving units are forbidden or have to be
noted in the database. Boxes within a shelving unit have individual numbers
so they can be found no matter where they are within the shelving unit. In
other, more "sleeping" areas, our location code is much more strict, sometimes even going down to individual places "front" and "back" on a single
pallet in a high storage rack.

Numbering individual shelves can have its pitfalls; if you use numbers,
there is a high risk of location confusion. You might start at the top with

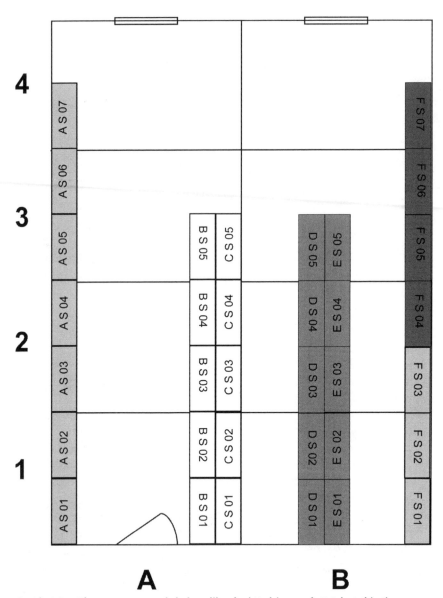

Graph 8.2. The same setup of shelves like depicted in graph 8.1 but this time numbered consistently

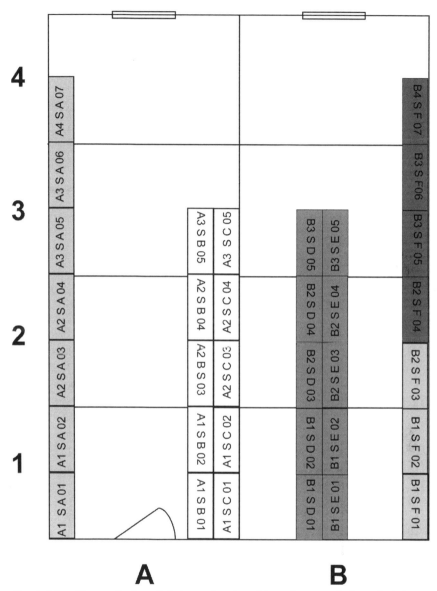

Graph 8.3. The numbering of shelves using the grid number as ordering principle.

"shelf 1" and number from there to the bottom, but someone else might think it's more logical that the bottom shelf is "shelf 1." You can avoid this if you label the shelves with letters, as the ReOrg methodology suggests.[7] But you will replace one issue with a similar one. While this methodology reasonably argues that you should work from bottom up, starting with "shelf a" as the lowest shelf, someone might assume that the top shelf is "shelf a" because you start reading a page from top down. This seems to be more intuitive with letters.

At the TECHNOSEUM we have worked a couple of times now with a system that uses the height of shelves as indicator. If we assume that the shelving unit is called "A S 01," the first shelf from the bottom would be "A S 01.005" because it is 5 inches above the ground, the next would be "A S 01.025," and so forth—the last shelf being maybe "A S 01.085." This holds the advantage that you can easily determine the right shelf, even without a tape measure. The difference between something being 5, 25, or 85 inches above the ground is easy to determine roughly, and no one would start measuring from the ceiling. An additional advantage comes if you have to move a whole collection, because you can easily determine how the shelving units and shelves have to be assembled in the new area. But this system also has its disadvantages: While you can easily add additional shelves it becomes problematic if you have to change the height of the existing shelves, because then you have to change the whole location name.

However you number your storage furniture, try to be concise and make sure everybody understands and can use the system. Mark all storage furniture with its exact location numbering and, if possible, mark the walls with their number or letter in your chessboard grid. It's a good idea to have a map of your location code visibly hung in your storage area. Also make sure that you have a procedure in place for changing locations. It has proven helpful to have two forms that state why and when an object was removed, by whom, and where it went. One of those forms goes to the one who changes the location in the database (who might be you) and from there into the object files, while the other one sits as a placeholder at the place the object was removed from.

COMMON MISTAKES

The possibilities of making mistakes are endless and as we will see in chapter 10, there is a way you can fail successfully. But it's also true that you don't have to repeat mistakes others made before you. Here are, in no particular order, some common storage mistakes:

- Storing too tight: Sure, space is valuable but if you cram your objects into one shelf in such a manner that you can't remove them safely, it does more harm than good. The same goes with too many objects in boxes.
- Overloading boxes: Keep a box's weight reasonable, otherwise the handles can break or someone can let the box slip because it's too heavy. As a rule of thumb, test the weight a number of times while packing. When you think the box is still reasonably light, take out a few objects because it's already too heavy. As you are lifting boxes all day long, you will always underestimate the actual weight.
- Playing Tetris[8] by finding ways for objects to fit into one another on a shelf, resulting in a maximum of packing density: This is a variation of the first mistake. Sure, handles or knobs can be cumbersome. You might save some space by placing objects in a way that the handle of the object in front blocks the way to an object deeper on the shelf, but this will almost inevitably cause damage when you try to remove the object behind the object with the handle. And, of course, that you never, ever stack objects in long-term storage should go without saying.
- Storing one-way: This is often encountered on the top shelves. Sure, one person can manage to shove an object onto the top shelf by pushing it from beneath. But to take it down from there without risking it being damaged, you will need two people on two ladders. A variation of this is shoving an object under the bottom shelf in such a way that you can only retrieve it by pulling it out, which most likely causes damage. Just don't do it! Find better solutions.
- Creating a *U* with shelving units: It seems like you can add an additional shelving unit in your master plan by forming a *U* at the end of two rows against a wall. In reality, the only space you gain is one you can't really use properly: you create corners that are difficult to number in your location system and nearly impossible to reach once the shelving units are filled with objects.
- Storing objects directly on the floor: The floor is no storage space. Objects belong on a shelf or on pallets. Storing on the floor holds a serious risk of objects being kicked, damaged by dollies, flooded by water, or damaged by condensation on uninsulated floors.
- Using aisles as storage space: Aisles are there to get to the objects and to allow everyday collections work as well as emergency evacuation—both for people and objects. Aisles are not places to store objects. They are not places to store objects temporarily. They are not places to store objects for a short time of just a day or two. They are not places to store boxes and crates for the next exhibition project. They just aren't.

STORAGE IMPROVEMENT IS NEVER DONE

As already stated at the beginning of this chapter storage improvement never ends. There is always some better method of storing and of course there are the occasional bigger and smaller catastrophes that lead to repacking and refurbishing. Then, there is the time you discover that some storage material that was considered "best practice" in the past actually damaged the stored objects and you have to replace the storage material. Finally, an active collections strategy of your museum will sooner or later lead to storage issues that only can be resolved by better storage furniture or a new storage area altogether.

So storage improvement will be your partner as long as you work with this collection—as will insufficient funds, so let's take a look at what to do if you can't afford to do anything.[9]

NOTES

1. Alex Dawson, ed., *Benchmarks in Collections Care for Museums, Archives and Libraries.* London: Museums, Archives and Libraries Council, 2011.

2. "Chapter 7: Museum Collection Storage," *NPS Museum Handbook*, Part I, *Museum Collections* (Washington, DC: National Park Service, 1990, chapter 7 updated 2012).

3. Scott Carrlee, "Caring for the Future: Collections Care Basics," in *Stewardship: Collections and Historic Preservation*, Book 6, *Small Museum Toolkit*, eds. Cinnamon Catlin-Legutko and Stacy Klingler (Lanham, MD: AltaMira Press, 2012), 1–41.

4. Ibid., p. 1

5. "Chapter 7: Museum Collection Storage," 7:1.

6. Rebecca A. Buck and Jean Allmann Gilmore, *Museum Registration Methods*, 5th ed. (MRM5) (Washington, DC: The AAM Press, 2010), p. 294.

7. Cultural Heritage Division of UNESCO, ed., *Methodology and Didactic Tools for Re-Organizing Museum Storage*, 2009, p. 99 ff.. http://unesdoc.unesco.org/images/0018/001862/186244e.pdf.

8. Tetris is a computer game whose objective is to fit blocks of different sizes and shapes into dense packing, preferably without any holes.

9. "Collections Care: What to Do When You Can't Afford to Do Anything" is a very thoughtful article written by Lisa Mibach in 1991 but unfortunately never published. However, you can always get a copy of it if you write to Lisa at lm@heritagepres.net

Chapter Nine

We Had Nothing

Having no money is not the exception but the norm for many museum collections. The repair bill that decreases the budget that was scheduled to buy some desperately needed archival boxes, or the just-cleaned objects becoming dusty again because there is no way to pay for the polyethylene bags are well-known issues, even in larger museums. How do you get the three important *m*'s: money, material, and manpower? Although scarcity of resources is not an issue that will go away easily, the first step doesn't cost anything: you have to learn to ask the right questions.

ASKING THE RIGHT QUESTIONS

When you work as a collections professional in a larger museum, you usually have a reasonable budget and are also in a comfortable position when it comes to knowledge about preservation needs. You can research what brand archival packaging and storage furniture is best suited for your object. When you are in doubt about what to do with the climate conditions in your storage area or how to treat an issue with an object you will probably have specialists on staff or you can hire one from outside the institution.

As the only collections specialist within the next few hundred miles, you have to take a different approach. You have to educate yourself about what harms the objects and what keeps them safe. Like knowing what to buy and where, this knowledge can't stay superficial. You have to understand the physical and chemical processes that lead to deterioration and what stops them or at least slows down those processes. You have to understand what makes archival material suitable for long-term storage. You will probably have to work with substitutes before you got money for "real" archival material, but you have to make sure that those substitutes don't do more harm than good. Probably all suppliers, craftsmen and even volunteers will tell you that what they suggest in either products or building improvements is absolutely safe for your collection. But the one who has to decide if this is true is you. That's why you have to learn to ask the right questions.

When packing an object, those questions will be something like, "How can off-gassing of plywood damage this material (and my health) and to what extent?" "What harm does an acidic cardboard box present if I use it to pack this object?" "What damages this carpet more: if I fold it and put it into the small archival box I have on hand or if I wrap it around this acidic cardboard tube I got for free at the local hardware store?" When it comes to your storage area it will be questions like, "Does it make sense to replace the old windows with new ones? Or are the old, not-so-tight ones that allow air circulation responsible for the relatively stable climate we have in the storage room at the moment and do I risk mold if they are replaced by new ones?" "Should I take the metal shelving units offered for free by a local chemical company or is there a risk that something toxic was previously stored on them that could harm the objects or the people working with the collection? Is there a method to check them?" Or, "Does it make sense to seek funding for a HVAC system or is there another way to keep the climate fluctuations to an acceptable minimum?"

You have some help, though. Through the "Power of Coffee" you will have built a strong network of people with special knowledge and can turn to them when in doubt. Online networks like the AAM junction, the RCAAM listserv, or the Connecting to Collections Care network are places to present possible solutions and discuss if you have overlooked something that harms your objects. However, to get valuable answers you have to ask precise questions. "How do I store carpets?" will produce answers with brand names, literature, and links to the same websites about storage solutions you may have already found yourself. "Is it acceptable to store a carpet on an acidic cardboard tube if I put a layer of polyethylene film between the cardboard and the carpet?" will produce much more helpful answers.

WRITING GRANT APPLICATIONS

Certainly the first thing that comes to mind if you think about how to acquire money for your collection is a grant. For researching what grants may be available contact your regional museum association and take a look at http://www.grants.gov/ to search for federal grant opportunities. As has happened so many times before, using the "Power of Coffee" might let you hear about

Figure 9.1. Parts of the collection of the Valdez Museum in Alaska before the cataloging and re-housing project, 2008, Courtesy of the Valdez Museum, Alaska.

grants or other funding possibilities that are only regional and not widely known. As Janice Klein points out, "some grants go unused while others have too many applicants."[1]

The effort it takes to apply for a grant is often underestimated. Keep in mind that some larger institutions have a member on staff who devotes a great deal of his or her working time on writing grant applications. Considering your working setup, this means that you have to decide carefully which grants you want to apply for, because as the sole collections professional, your time is limited. The lottery method—applying for many grants, even if they only remotely fit your purpose, in order to increase the likeliness of getting one approved—is seldom a good strategy. Instead, choose grants that match your own collection care, documentation, and/or storage improvement strategy best. Then, invest the time necessary to write a really good application. Begin the writing process early and watch the deadline. I mean it: watch the deadline! Deadlines are a lot like objects in a mirror: They are closer than they appear. Before you know it, they are already there or even past. That's especially problematic with grants because grant funds can decrease, the pool of potential applications might increase, and there is no guarantee that the same grant is available next year. So, make sure that you have a safety grid of reminders: alerts on your computer and markers in your calendar, and you might even assign a friend to remind you a week before the deadline.

Keep in mind that the professionals who make the grant award decisions often have the same tight schedule and backbreaking workload as you. In addition they receive dozens or hundreds of applications for a single grant. Except for some rare cases, all of these suggested projects are worth getting funded. Your task is to give them a reason why they should fund *your* project instead of all the others. You can't actively influence their decisions, but you can make their work a lot easier, increasing the likeliness that your application doesn't land on the "no" stack too early. Here are a few suggestions:

1. Follow the rules. While being the only museum professional within the next hundred miles often means that you have to be creative and sometimes bend or even break some rules to reach your goals, grant writing isn't the place to do it. Make sure you've read and understood all the formal requirements before you apply. Apply only if you fulfill all those requirements. If you are supposed to use a form provided, use it and complete it accordingly. If you have additional comments or something you want the committee to know about your project that doesn't fit into the form, list them in the "remarks" section or, if there isn't such a section, add them in a separate letter.

2. Be meticulous. In the normal madness of everyday catastrophes, writing grant applications is often delayed, sometimes hastily written in a "last minute panic" mode the night before the closing date. Obviously that's not the best way to do it. You wouldn't do it that way if it were your application for a job you really wanted, would you? Well, a grant is very much like a job application. If your salary for the next year is dependent on getting the grant approved, it actually *is* a job application. So be careful, avoid grammar and spelling mistakes, let it lie for a day or two before you read it again for corrections and, if possible, send it to a friend to critically read it. A committee that is swamped with grant applications will be happy to sort one out because it screams "sloppy project manager" to them.

3. Make it easy to understand your project. You probably wouldn't invest money in a project that seems vague and somehow not thoroughly thought through. Well, neither would grant committees. Make sure you outline your project plan in a logical, easy-to-understand way. State what you need the funding for and how you will use the money.

4. Have your facts and figures straight. When listing what you will need the money for, be as precise as possible. If you calculated the costs for storage furniture or archival material, list those prices. If you want to install an

HVAC system, list prices for the equipment and for installation. If you calculated man-hours, give the committee an idea of how you calculated them—for example, that you packed and moved a sample shelving unit to calculate the man-hours needed for the storage move. The grant money comes mostly from public sources or associations, so it is either tax money or membership fees. You want that money to be spent on a proper calculation, not on some vague figures from out of the blue.

5. Be prepared to follow through. If you are awarded the grant, make sure that you can really undertake this project before you accept it. This is a contract, if they give you the money, you have to spend it all on items outlined in your application, not for something else. Be prepared to document how you spent it and to be held responsible if you fail to follow through. Don't forget to take pictures before, during, and after the project!

FINDING SUPPORTERS

In a large collection the things you can do yourself to help your collection might end with writing grant applications. In a really large institution, you might even end up suggesting which grants to apply for, but not actually having control over if it happens or not. In a small institution there's more opportunity to get creative. You can actively try to search out supporters for your collection care endeavors. There is an excellent resource called *Capitalize on Collections Care* by the Heritage Preservation in Partnership with the Institute for Museum and Library Services that gives you some ideas about what could be done.[2]

The most important thing to understand—and the most difficult fact to swallow for any long-term, dyed-in-the-wool, collections professional—is that protecting our cultural heritage for generations to come is a far too abstract goal for most people, at least too abstract for someone to lay out any money for. If you want people to donate money or purchase archival materials for you, you have to engage them. To say it simply: you need to find something that is either fun or prestigious to give money for; preferably it's both. Here are a few ideas:

- A Tale of an Object: You probably discovered a whole bunch of good stories in your collection that you can tell by the objects. This is a great starting point for engaging people. Tell the story and people will relate to it and maybe have their own stories that relate to it. That's a great conversation starter for explaining how you want to preserve this story and the object for future generations and that you need funding to do that. Possible ways

Figure 9.2. The same collection as seen in 9.1 after the cataloging and re-housing project, 2008, the cataloging internship was made possible by a grant from the Alaska State Museum. Courtesy of the Valdez Museum, Alaska.

to communicate those stories include guided tours, pop-up exhibitions, lectures, local newspaper articles, and/or your blog/website.
• Conservation in Progress: While most people are easily bored by tales about long-term preservation and documentation, most people also love to see conservation treatment of an object. It has a certain dynamic and the good fairytale ending "happy ever after." That's a peg on which you can hang your fund-raising. There are identified objects that need conserva-

tion treatment, so define this as the goal of your fund-raising campaign. Understand that part of giving is that people want to see what is done with their money, so find a way for people who are donating to see the progress that is being made. This could be regular updates in the local newspapers or on your website or a look in the conservator's workshop for donors on some special occasions. Make sure that people understand that the storage situation is crucial for the conserved object to survive "happily ever after" and that you need part of the money to improve object storage and/or to buy archival materials.

- Adopt an Artifact: This is a similar approach to those already mentioned, but in this case an individual decides to give money for one special object, thus creating a special relationship. In return, the donor can be mentioned on the label when the object is exhibited or get some other kind of recognition that thanks him or her for being the friend and caretaker of this object.
- Give to Get: The reciprocal of "Adopt an Artifact." In this case you organize an event that doesn't necessarily have anything to do with your museum or the collection. The idea is that the revenue, or part of the revenue will go to your collection to improve the storage situation, to buy archival material, storage furniture, and so forth. The possibilities are endless: lectures; concerts; a festival where all cake, chili, and salads are gifts of citizens; a museum party with a raffle; a stew day where visitors pay $10 for a bowl of stew ($2 for the actual stew and $8 as a donation to the collection). There are hundreds of possibilities and the best might not yet have seen the light of day. The big advantage of this method is that you can attract people who are not typically interested in the exhibitions and collections of your museum. Who doesn't love cake and music, after all? The disadvantage is that these events are the most time consuming, might cost money in advance, and you definitely need others to help, while you can put the first three ideas into effect all by yourself (although having assistance never hurts).

Whatever you do, keep in mind that money doesn't just knock on your door. In order to get money for the collection, you have to invest time. Nowadays there are a few tools, like the Internet platform Kickstarter and others, that make it a bit easier to raise money for your cause. However, they are just tools; the work must still be done by someone. And, like so many times before, it is very likely that this someone is you. You have to schedule enough of your time for these projects and skip other tasks in favor of them. Fund-raising is nothing that can be done in the evening hours after a whole day of work. While you might meet a potential donor at your local pub after work, this should not be the norm. Invest normal working time for planning and organizing your campaigns carefully and make sure that the workload doesn't crush you. There are some fund-raising ideas that might sound great on paper, but when thinking about the amount of work involved, you might come to the conclusion that they just aren't feasible. I remember one museum sending individually engraved memory plates to everybody who donated a certain amount of money. It turned out that the costs for engraving, packing, and shipping were pretty high and if you counted the hours that staff had to invest in keeping this project on track, there wasn't much revenue left.

Having helping hands is always great and in fund-raising, they are nearly indispensable. Especially if you are more on the introversion spectrum (which is not that uncommon for collections people, the author included) you might try to find someone who just lives and breathes for meeting people and asking them for their support. This is a great chance for a volunteer who is all

---

A REAL-WORLD EXAMPLE

We sponsored an "Adopt an Artifact" program years ago at the Fredericksburg Area Museum and Cultural Center in Fredericksburg, Virginia. We identified about a dozen objects that needed to have conservation or repair work done. Working with conservators, we got estimates on what it would cost to do the work, as well as basic treatment proposals. The cover story of our newsletter that summer was all about "Adopt An Object, Preserve the Past." We featured the objects in need of work (including photos), talked about the importance of conservation and how many things come to museums in need of work, how expensive this work can be, and then gave the cost estimate of what it would take. People were encouraged to contact me if they were interested and then I could give them particulars about what the conservation of that piece entailed. We had pretty good success—about half of the objects were sponsored. The money came in and was put in a restricted fund so it could only be used for what the donor intended. We got the object on the conservator's schedule of work and then paid for it out of the fund when the work was complete. Those objects now have two credit lines when used in exhibitions or publications—the one for the original donor and the one for the person who sponsored the conservation.

Mary Helen Dellinger
Curator
Manassas Museum, Manassas, Virginia

thumbs with handling objects but great with people. Or this might be a task for an organization that isn't directly involved with your museum—the local boy scouts pack, your church community, the local quilt club—sometimes organizations that are used to collecting money more than you are might offer a helping hand for a special project. But, of course, you have to use a little of that "Power of Coffee" to persuade them.

UNLEASH YOUR CREATIVITY

If you were ever a student or a freelancer or had a part-time museum job that required many more than the hours written in your contract, you are possibly a master of the ancient martial art of making ends meet. You are probably familiar with lingering around the bakery at closing time to get a loaf of bread for a bargain price or using your unique abilities as a computer wizard in exchange for someone's helping you repaint your apartment. Seeing chances for collaboration and thinking about available materials and skills is what you need if you have to manage a collection without much money. As this has to do with using creativity, there is no fixed path to show you. I can only write down a few ideas I have already used in the past and that might work for you. But this list is neither complete nor exclusive, and there is no guarantee that any of these suggestions will work in your special case:

• Who manufactures this? As I already stressed at the beginning of this chapter not all the material you need must be necessarily archival. Try to find out where else a certain material is used and if it is interchangeable with the material normally used in the museum context. This goes for tools and gloves as well as certain storage furniture and packing materials. Just make sure you check all the specifications before you bring something to your collection. Before I took the job at the TECHNOSEUM one of the curators bought a decent amount of plastic bags for protecting her collection against dust. Some years later it turned out that these bags were compostable and to this day we still find little pieces of those decomposed plastic bags in some remote areas of our storage or, worse, inside of objects. Moral of this story: if you are not 100 percent sure that those materials don't harm your collection, don't use them.

• You don't need that anymore? Sometimes another institution wants to get rid of equipment they can't use anymore. Shelving units, crates, boxes—sometimes even professional literature. Keep watching the professional listservs and websites and you might get really useful things with only having to pay for the shipping.

A REAL-WORLD EXAMPLE

Our library disposed of their old cabinets used for storing magazines. After a quick check, we decided to reuse them in our storage. They provide a nearly dust-free series of compartments for our collection of pressing irons. Each compartment holds up to two pressing irons.

Figure 9.3. Storage of the collection of pressing irons in an old library cabinet, March 2015, TECHNOSEUM, Foto Hans Bleh

- The test sample: Manufacturers are sometimes open to giving away a free test sample of some of their archival materials. Ask for it.
- A few rolls more? If you are already planning a fund-raising event for archival materials, ask if the manufacturer is willing to sponsor the event. Adding a few rolls or boxes for free to your order might be easier than donating money. You might also try to negotiate a certain bargain deal: if you manage to find enough supporters to buy one hundred archival boxes, the manufacturer will donate another one hundred.
- We can fix it: Your local roofer might be more willing to volunteer a few free hours working time than to donate money. Or he or she might even do the job pro bono if allowed to put an advertisement sign on your roof.

- You're welcome: Your local construction company might be happy to lend you their dehumidifiers free of charge for a certain period of time when they won't need them elsewhere. It doesn't cost them much more than a smile—and you only have to calculate the electricity costs to bring your storage area to a dryer state. Warning: make sure you don't dry it too quickly and that dehumidifying that area does indeed make sense.
- The Paperwork Fairy: Helping a local shop owner to sort out all the paperwork needed for shipping a large order abroad might be worth a donation to your collection to him or her.

These are just a few ideas. Try to find out what works best for your institution and in your community using the "Power of Coffee."

THE STORY NEVER ENDS

At times we all dream about the white knight aka the mystical donor who comes out of the blue and relieves us of all our money troubles. In reality this seldom happens and as long as Murphy's Law is still in place, it won't happen to a small historical collection in the boonies where one single museum professional trics to bring his or her collection to an acceptable state. Instead, looking for money will be as much an ongoing task as improving your storage, collections care, and documentation strategy. As soon as the first money comes in you must take care of completing the reports for the grant association, informing your donors about the conservation progress, and writing Christmas cards to those who adopted an artifact. The list goes on and on. While you pack your first archival boxes you will already have drafted in your mind the application for the next grant. And while you patiently try to convince a major donor that he simply cannot have a party in the storage area for his friends, even if one of his friends is a celebrity, you might feel the sudden urge to hug the development officer at your former museum (with whom you had serious disputes) because now, finally, you see her side of the story.

You won't always get the grant approved and your fund-raising campaign might earn you less revenue than you expected. Sometimes you win, sometimes you lose. So in the next chapter, let us take a look at failures—real ones—and failures that aren't really failures.

NOTES

1. This remark and many other useful tips on grants can be found in a newsletter article called "Small Museum Friendly Grants" by Janice Klein in *Big Ideas for Small*

Museums: The AASLH Small Museums Affinity Group Newsletter 2 (February 2011), http://www.mynewsletterbuilder.com/email/newsletter/1410719137.

2. *Capitalize on Collections Care,* Heritage Preservation, available for free download at http://www.heritagepreservation.org/PDFS/COClo.pdf.

Chapter Ten

Failing Successfully

You all know the old adage that we must learn from our mistakes and I'm certain we all strive to do this. It is obviously not smart to make the same mistake twice and so, throughout the book, I have tried to point you to common mistakes several people have made when managing an unmanaged collection, so you can learn from their mistakes instead of repeating them. It's also true that when you are doing something, chances are that you are doing something wrong. That's nothing to be angry or depressed about; when you realize you did something wrong, just make it right the next time. But there are two aspects of failure you should be aware of: the first, that sometimes failure is an option; and second, that it isn't failure if a plan isn't working the way you have expected. Not recognizing both could endanger your project or worse, yourself.

SOMETIMES, FAILURE IS AN OPTION

If you ever saw the 1995 movie *Apollo 13*, you probably loved the moment when the flight director Gene Kranz turns to his team, who have to use their collective knowledge and creativity to bring the three astronauts safely back to earth, and states, "Failure is not an option!" In a way, *"Failure is not an option!"* is also the main topic of this book, as I tried to point out that there is always a way to improve the situation of an unmanaged collection, even if you lack money, staff, and material. However, there is a difference between boldly going against the odds and uselessly fighting for a cause that is obviously lost. A firefighter that runs into a burning house can be either courageous or careless. Courageous, if he figured out that there is an ever-so-slight chance to rescue the people inside if he just acts fast now, without waiting for backup. Careless, when the house is close to collapsing and he goes in there without safety apparatus, taking the risk of being buried himself, and probably risking the lives of his comrades who will have to go in there to save him.

The good news is that in managing unmanaged collections the decisions are not that dramatic most of the time and the outcome, not that lethal. However, given the fact that you only have your health and one lifetime it can be crucial to assess, every now and then, whether you are just pursuing a difficult-to-achieve goal or if you are wasting your energy and it is time to cease this project. At the end of chapter 4 we discussed such a possible scenario: If your storage conditions are such that you will never be able to reach a climate where mold is not an issue and there is no chance of sourcing an alternative storage area with better conditions, it's useless to invest your time in treating the mold. And it's careless to keep on documenting this collection if you don't have money to buy protective equipment for yourself and your staff. There are a lot of similar situations—storage below the waterline that is flooded every springtime and no one in upper management is willing to do something about it, a museum that is so poorly funded that they are not able to pay your wages or your bills, a collection so badly damaged that there is no way to save it—to name but a few.

Other unwinnable situations might not be that obvious and you might need the point of view of an outsider like a friend, family member, or friendly board member to help you see the uselessness of your efforts. Those situations might have to do with personal constellations. In chapter 6, I pointed out the fact that sometimes a great constellation of people can lead to outstanding results, against all odds. Unfortunately, there are also unlucky constellations that have the opposite effect: although it should thrive considering the available resources, the project is stuck.

If you have a director or mayor who has serious prejudices against recent graduates from Museum Studies programs, females with a PhD, collections managers without a PhD, farmer's daughters from Kentucky, or men with red hair, your best ideas might be rejected without your seeing the real reason. Prejudices are terrible, but as they are part of our human nature, it's hard to go against them. My perception is that they are the easier to overcome the more you work together. When you are handling artifacts, stacking boxes, and take measurements together, it's nearly impossible to stay prejudiced against one another. If all are willing to achieve a common goal and are open to trying to work together, prejudices go away. You might still dislike a colleague, but this time because of certain personal traits, not because of his or her background.

It's much more difficult if the prejudice is held by someone in upper management. Because they don't work closely with you, it's easier for them to see all your suggestions with their own prejudice in mind and might reject them when they would have easily agreed to them were they made by someone else. Sometimes the reason for the rejection of good suggestions is not due to prejudice, but personal friction. Upper management's not liking your working style or the way you speak has the same outcome as prejudices and there is not much you can do about it. Sometimes you might find a way to work around those issues by finding someone else—a community member who knows the director well, a board member, or a respected volunteer—to make those suggestions and move the project forward. But sometimes it's just a no-win situation, both for you and the collection. And that's one of those cases where ceasing the project is the only healthy way to deal with it.

When you come to the conclusion that this is a situation you can't go against and you have to cease this project, it's important to finish strong. Just because you failed doesn't mean that this is the ultimate result for the collection. There might come a time when someone donates a large sum of money to manage the collection, there might be a change in upper management, or someone might take over who has better ideas on how to proceed. There might even come a time when you can take the project up again because the conditions have changed for the better. So it's important to tie up all the loose ends. Document everything you have done so far and never burn bridges. If you were consistent in keeping your diary as suggested in chapter 3, this shouldn't be too difficult to do. Make sure that your last entry states why you have decided to cease the project and what you would have done next if things had turned out differently. Concerning the collection, make sure your successor can easily find where you left off—that is, mark the row, the shelving unit and the shelf where you stopped documenting. Make sure all documents are properly filed and easy to find. If you have reached a logical exit as suggested in chapters 3–7, state which exit was reached. Make sure you tell various people where they can find the files in case someone else takes over. Lastly, write a note to upper management that once more outlines what you've done so far, where you left off, and what should be done next with the collection. Also state where they can find all documents concerning the collection. Even if no one reads this letter, chances are this letter is filed somewhere and will be found by whoever takes over.

Even if you are not at all in the mood to be kind to your prospective successors, you should make the effort. Beyond all practical use, this is a form of paying respect to your own work. Whatever happened and however sad the situation is, by tying up the loose ends you make sure that this project is not a complete failure. All you have done is well documented and whoever takes over in the future will not have to start from zero again as you had to do. That way, years later you can think about this project with your head held high. You improved this collection's situation and you acted professionally right to the end.

CHANGING PLANS IS NOT FAILURE

There is another aspect not covered sufficiently in currently available literature. Throughout this book we have laid out several plans and strategies. This gives the impression that you make a plan and then you follow through until it's finished. While that is the ideal, I have never ever seen it work that way. In fact, reality and Mother Nature could not care less about your strategy. Things will happen that will require you to change your plans and adapt to the changed situation. It is a problem that this aspect of our work isn't part of our training as museum professionals. Because we learn how to make plans and strategies, but not how to adapt to all the things that happen while we try to put them into effect, we tend to try to shape reality so it fits to our plan instead of adapting the plan. Needless to say, this does not work; but it's astounding how often you see someone trying to do just this. The issue is that because we don't learn that the adaption process is just as important as the planning process, we tend to see it as a personal failure if a plan doesn't work out. It's not failure, it's a principle!

Mind me, I'm not talking about plans that are destined to fail the very moment they are written down. Plans that only work out under ideal circumstances are not worth the ink on the paper. A schedule that only works if every supplier delivers and every craftsman finishes on time, a storage improvement strategy that only works if you get one special grant approved, an exhibition opening that can only take place if none of the volunteers (or, in fact, one particular volunteer) is ever sick; all these are examples of useless plans. Every plan has to contain a certain amount of buffer in staff, time, and money. If it doesn't, the plan can cause chaotic situations, such as truck loads of objects arriving before the space this collection should be stored in is cleared, volunteers who have nothing to do because the shelving units they should install didn't arrive on time, part of the collection doesn't fit into the newly built storage units because the space needs weren't properly estimated. The possibilities are endless. The results of such poor planning are seldom acknowledged but along with the obvious less-than-ideal end result come unnecessary overtime hours, a tense working environment, work accidents, and objects are being damaged because staff is pressed for time or there simply isn't enough space to store the objects without damage. Those "plans" are not plans in the real sense of the word; they are wishful thinking, and if they don't work, it's not a failure. It's natural and a sign of careless project management.

Instead I'm talking about plans as carefully crafted as I hope your documentation, collections care, and storage improvement strategy are. While putting them into effect, life will get in your way. You are not getting a certain grant, your fund-raiser raises less money than expected, a heavy storm destroys your roof, the board member who is an enthusiastic advocate of collections work retires and your can-do-everything craftsman and adviser Paul moves out of country. Whatever happens, you have to adapt.

In my working life I encountered two types of successful project managers: the first type I like to call the "obsessive compulsive" or "anticipating" type, who in a nearly compulsive manner likes to have everything under control, thinks about all possible outcomes beforehand, and finds a solution for them in advance. He or she has anticipated all kinds of hindering circumstances to their plan beforehand and has already thought through what they could do if this happens. The other one I like to call the "creative" type. He or she does less to try to anticipate possible catastrophes, but has a talent for improvisation and quickly finding alternative solutions in case of emergency.

This example shows the difference: If a pipe bursts in storage, the anticipating type will pull out of a pocket the telephone number of a plumber with 24/7 service and one for the cold storage facility with which the museum has a contract in case of emergency. Next he or she will call all staff members and volunteers who have gone through the yearly emergency preparedness training and organize the evacuation of the collection and the transport of the objects that got wet to the cold storage facility. The creative type thrown into the same situation will call the local hardware shop owner to ask him or her for all the plastic containers he has in stock and call all the people he or she knows in the vicinity to organize an evacuation of the collection.

Really good project managers are always a mixture of both types. They might tend to be either more anticipating or more creative, but they will all have an emergency preparedness plan and be able to find creative solutions on the spot.

There's one thing that all good project managers have in common: they stay calm and never react in haste. They allow themselves a few minutes to think about the situation and consider all options before they give any orders.

I remember the day before the great opening of *Elementa 1*, a new permanent exhibition of the TECHNOSEUM that, for the first time in Europe, combined science center elements with real historical objects, showing not only the physical objects, but also how they are used in real life. Needless to say, all were running around, in a last minute panic, fixing and adjusting things. All? Well, not the project manager. When the director asked him, "You are so calm. Aren't you nervous at all?" the project manager just calmly replied, "What good does it do if I'm nervous?"

For me, that's the essence of good project management. It doesn't help if you are nervous and worried if your plan doesn't work out the way you thought. There is no use in panicking, less use in laying the blame on oneself or, worse, on someone else. Just stay calm and consider your options. To continue with the previous example, when there is a burst pipe and the storage area is flooded, the good project manager, no matter what type, will first of all think of where the main tap is and if he or she can get to it without risk, considering the possibility of the electrical installation's being affected by the water in the storage. If he or she deems it safe, the project manager will first of all turn off the water. Otherwise, this person will first ensure that the electricity for the building is shut down. The project manager will never risk anything, may it be the life of a colleague or just that something is done the wrong way, by being hasty with decisions.

So be prepared to adapt all your neatly laid-out strategies and plans several times in the process. You may not get the funding for the next step in your storage improvement strategy, so this year you devote all your working time to documentation and housekeeping. You may run so severely out of money that you have to put all your efforts into fund-raising before you can even think of continuing with further collections care. You may already be close to the fourth logical exit when one night a tree hits your storage area and you basically have to start all over again. These are not failures! These are things that happen, and you just adapt and keep going.

CELEBRATE—YOUR FAILURES
AS WELL AS YOUR SUCCESSES

When you've accepted that there is a time when failure *is* an option and you understand that a change in plan is not a failure, you are still left with those things you did incorrectly. A miscalculation of needed storage space, an important data entry you forgot to integrate into your documentation strategy, a storage layout that isn't in accordance with fire regulations. The possibilities are endless. No matter how you look at it, you simply messed up. You could kick yourself for hours or you could whistle and pretend it didn't happen; neither action helps. You only have one option: you have to own your mistake. You have to analyze what went wrong and why and find a solution to the issue your mistake caused. But there is also one thing you should do to help the people involved and you to get over it: Celebrate it!

In a long and at times stressful process such as managing an unmanaged collection, you should never underestimate the importance of working in some type of distraction from the day-to-day worries. One possibility is

A REAL-WORLD EXAMPLE

We prepared an exhibition exclusively from our collection of electrical household appliances at the TECHNOSEUM. Our aim was to show not all, but at least a great number, of the objects we have on this topic. And we wanted to give our visitors an impression of what it is like in one of our storage areas, so instead of showcases, we used our everyday shelving units.

Our whole schedule was based upon preparing this exhibition beforehand in our storage area. We meticulously laid out every presentation in an example shelving unit, carefully arranged the objects, documented their position on the shelves, and packed and labeled our packing cases accordingly. Our plan was that during the installation of the exhibition it wouldn't be necessary for someone involved in the preparation process to be present all the time. Instead, anybody with basic training in art handling would be able to install this exhibition according to our project documentation. That way, even if the whole team had been run over by a bus or if we had had less time for installation than scheduled, we would have been able to open the exhibition right on time.

We were working on the final seven of seventy-six shelving units when one day a colleague (who wasn't directly involved with the

Figure 10.1. Presenting objects in a slight angle was one way to avoid presentations looking crammed, foto Bernd Kießling

preparation of the exhibition) passed by and said, "You know that these aren't the shelving units that will be in the exhibition?" I was in a shock. It turned out that we had based our whole arrangements on shelves that were exactly 18 cm (about 7 inches) wider than the shelves we would have in the exhibition.

When we analyzed what happened, it was again a shock. The department head had ordered a colleague to "set up the example shelving unit." Unfortunately it turned out that there were two kinds of shelves: 160 cm (63 inches) wide and 178 cm (70 inches) wide. Normally, the wider ones should only fit into the posts that are 4 m (157 inches) high, but because of an unusual coincidence, they also fit into the posts for the smaller shelves that were 2 m (79 inches) high. My colleague didn't know that there were different shelves; he took the posts with the right height and assembled them with (what seemed to him) shelves that fit. But that wasn't his fault. The real mistake came when I didn't check the measurement of the complete example shelving unit before starting with the preparation process. I knew exactly how wide the shelves had to be, relied on my visual judgment that told me they were the right shelves, and didn't double-check with a tape measure. I goofed up.

After we found out what happened, we called it a day, bought a couple of beers, and clinked our glasses "to 18 centimeters!" We wouldn't have produced anything useful anymore that day. The next day, we

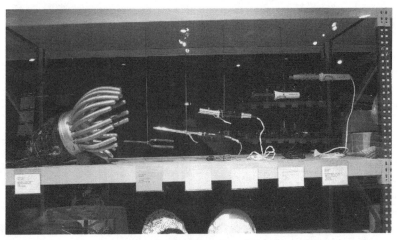

Figure 10.2. The "swimming curling irons" and the "octopus" (in reality an appliance to make permanent waves) became a visitor's favorite, foto Bernd Kießling

went back to work, corrected the example shelving unit, and developed a packing and return transport procedure for those objects not fitting on the shelves, which would become obvious during installation. In the aftermath, this failure turned out to be rather inspirational: instead of just following the original layout the team had to unleash its creativity when trying to fit as many objects as possible on the shelves without the layout's looking crammed.

to celebrate small successes. A ritual dance when you reach certain accession numbers like 100, 500, or 3,333; a coffee break when you've found an object that matches with an old deed of gift; a cake for all when you have documented the last shelf of the last shelving unit in a row. Search for those little reasons to laugh and celebrate. Celebrating your mistakes is equally important. It avoids being dragged into the black hole of self-accusation. When working in a team, celebration creates an atmosphere of straightforwardly admitting mistakes and working together on improvements, instead of concealing them and talking about them behind the backs of others.

Talking and writing about managing unmanaged collections is rather easy; doing it is what really counts. So, let's take a look at some successful projects and the experiences of completing them.

Chapter Eleven

Success Stories

After reading a lot of theory about managing a previously unmanaged collection and looking at your own collection, you might like to know if there are people out there who actually succeeded in managing their collection. While there might not be many who proudly say that they have a perfectly managed collection, there are a lot of colleagues who successfully improved their collection. As you may have guessed, the author is one of them.

In 2004, when I took over the job as the collections manager at the Landesmuseum für Technik und Arbeit, later renamed the TECHNOSEUM, I already knew what to expect. Fulfilling a requirement for studying Museum Studies at the Fachhochschule für Technik und Wirtschaft (University of Applied Sciences) in Berlin, I had done a six-month internship in 1998 in this museum and had helped in cleaning and rehousing the typewriter collection and cataloged a collection of 400 tin cans. So, I knew what I had to expect was far from the best practices in collections management and preventive conservation I learned during my studies.

The collection, consisting of nearly everything that played a role in people's working and private lives since 1850, from a gramophone needle to a complete inland water vessel, was built up in the 1980s with much enthusiasm but little knowledge about handling and storing objects. Over the years things had piled up in three large industrial halls that served as storage areas. Action to improve the situation was taken years before I joined the team, so when I took up the job of the collections manager I could actually walk in the aisles and on some rare occasions an object was actually on the shelf where the database said it would be. However, there were many things to improve. It actually took the pressure of having to give up one of the three storage halls in 2005/2006 to get funding for better storage furniture and real archival packaging instead of begging for banana boxes from the nearby grocery store.

Figure 11.1. One of the three storage halls of the Landesmuseum für Technik und Arbeit, 1993, TECHNOSEUM, Foto Klaus Luginsland

We as a team had definitely what is sometimes referred to as a "steep learning curve," especially as most of the professional literature dealt with the preservation and storage of paintings and sculptures, not of plows and radios. With time, we developed many methods and procedures, which helped us a great deal when we adopted some large, previously unmanaged collections, like a collection of advertising material (2011, estimated 3,000 objects), electronic tubes (2012, 1,800 objects), and radio and broadcasting equipment (2014, estimated 5,800 objects), as well as revising and improving the documentation of our existing collection of cameras, tape and reel-to-reel recorders, TV sets, film and slide projectors and radios (2010/2011, about 2,000 objects), and electrical household equipment (2013/2014, about 3,000 objects).

Whenever we compared notes with colleagues from other institutions who also worked with a previously unmanaged collection, we discovered that we often had made the same mistakes in the beginning and wished someone had told us before. When it came to advising colleagues in smaller institutions with collections in peril, I often found it hard to pass on my knowledge in a structured, easy-to-understand way. I wished I could just hand them a book containing all that we had learned along the way, together with useful references so they could start off more professionally than we had. Well, now you know why you have this book in hand.

In a way, we were still lucky with our collection at the TECHNOSEUM: From the very beginning there was documentation—even if the connection

Figure 11.2. The same storage hall as depicted in 11.1 after installing heavy-duty racks, October 2012, TECHNOSEUM, Foto Hans Bleh

between the object and its documentation was often lost and the relationship was hard to reestablish, especially because the catalog entries were often very basic. But when I take a look at the success stories that were submitted by my colleagues for this last chapter of the book I thank my lucky stars that so far no tree hit my storage, no one glued some objects together to make a better display for storage tours, and while I had to remove the occasional dead mouse every now and then, I never had to walk over numbers of dead carcasses. While you read these stories you will recall many things you've read in the chapters and you will realize that while the challenges and collections were all very different, the work toward improvement has many similarities. I'm eternally grateful to all colleagues who were willing to step up and tell their stories in this book.

THE FLANNERY O'CONNOR—ANDALUSIA FOUNDATION

The Flannery O'Connor—Andalusia Foundation is dedicated to the restoration, preservation, and public interpretation of Andalusia Farm, the final home of Flannery O'Connor from 1951 until her death from lupus in 1964. This is where O'Connor was living when she completed her two novels and two collections of short stories and numerous essays, all important and influential contributions to twentieth-century literature. O'Connor's writings have been translated into many languages and have been made into plays, films, and other media, and her work enjoys a worldwide following. Visitors to Andalusia come from across the globe. Our visitor log includes entries from Rome and Paris, the U.K. and Canada, Iraq and Japan. These folks are joined by visitors from all over the United States.

The collection at this former dairy farm includes both nonliving collections (structures, furniture, household items, textiles, ephemera, and a panoply of materials related to the farming operation: everything ranging in scale from farm machinery to hundreds of hand-forged nails), and living collections (we steward over 500 hundred acres of woodland and pasture landscape, a gem in an increasingly developed corridor, and peafowl). There are twelve historic structures, most in varying degrees of disrepair from vulnerable to completely collapsed. The farm operation was closed in 1975, eleven years after the death of the writer in 1964. A nonprofit organization, established in 2001, now owns and manages the property. Open to the public, the farm receives over 5,000 visitors annually. To date, restoration and rehabilitation efforts have focused on the farm core and emergencies.

Andalusia Farm does not currently have a collections policy and there are numerous issues outstanding that need to be addressed (standards of care, hierarchy, interpretation, preservation and access, and ownership, etc.). That said, we recognize that developing a collections policy and clarifying some of the outstanding issues is an important and fundamental step in the organization's maturation and move toward increasing best practices. There's no inventory of even high-interpretive value items and there are some ownership questions that have never been resolved. A Gordian knot of collection issues!

About a month after I started, a tree fell on the Equipment Shed, a 3,200-square-foot, vernacular structure filled to capacity with one hundred years of farm tools and implements. The shed, already degraded by holes in the roof, is a prominent structure in the barnyard, key to the interpretation of life on the farm, and important for connecting O'Connor's fiction with the place that inspired it. A group of volunteers (farmers and country folk with machinery and know-how) was mobilized to help empty the shed of collection materials and move it to swing space in the large cow barn. On the first of four intense work days, the crew filled two 40-foot long tarps with about one third of the total material. Subsequent work days dealt with even more stuff: a wagon and tractor, many different types of plows and seeders, a huge and heavy roll of fencing, three cast iron sinks and a tub, machine parts galore, saddles, a chemical safe, even a bag of clothes). We documented what kinds of materials came from each of the bays so we could make an effort to recreate

Figure 11.3.   Farming objects saved from the destroyed equipment shack. Courtesy of Flannery O'Connor-Andalusia Foundation

this work space that was at the heart of farm operations when repair and reuse were the norm.

After some successful fundraising, Phase One of the rebuild is complete. We approached this work in the spirit of the original by using lumber harvested on-site and adopting the same simple construction evidenced in the original structure. This, after a visit to the SHPO (state historic preservation officer) and confirmation that using private funds to rebuild this structure in-kind would not run afoul of our status on the National Register of Historic Places. The good news is we have received funding for Phase Two. Upon completion the rebuilt shed will serve as sheltered program space in the rear, open shed area, thereby quadrupling our current capacity for only twenty-five people inside the house. This area will be handicapped accessible while the house is not. The front of the structure, facing the barnyard, will recreate the look of the farm during the period of significance, mid-twentieth century. Phase Three will return materials to the bays they are associated with (forge area, machine shop, tack room, etc.) and will be interpreted as part of the visitor experience. One bay will be converted to composting toilets, allowing for handicapped accessible facilities to supplement the main house's single (non-ADA) toilet, the only one on-site.

The main house where O'Connor and her mother lived (with weekend visits by Uncle Louis who co-owned the farm with Mrs. O'Connor) is a nineteenth-century farm house without air-conditioning. For close to a decade one of the upstairs rooms—packed to capacity plus some— has been closed and locked. Ownership of the material is not clear. However what did become clear was that we were experiencing a rat problem. They chewed through wires on our fire and security system causing it to randomly trigger, in turn triggering arrival of local police and the volunteer fire department multiple times. Not good. There was no evidence of rats anywhere else in the house, so we figured they must be having a party up there.

So the first step was to empty the room. We pulled everything out onto the front lawn to air out and take a cursorily look at what was there. A crew of five strapping young men spent hours bringing out furniture, clothes, farm records, kitchen items, and so forth. We took photos of items as best we could and determined what was not going into off-site storage—namely old mattresses that served as home for the vermin. These materials headed to the landfill. We now have everything off-site in roomy-enough storage bins so we can work with family members to determine disposition. The farm house room is now clear. We have erected free-standing shelving and are starting to use the room as curatorial work space as we start to sort through other materials found under the laundry room sink downstairs: Uncle Louis's papers, empty envelopes addressed to the writer, books, and, in mint condition,

Figure 11.4.   The upstairs room where the rat infestation was detected. Courtesy of Flannery O'Connor-Andalusia Foundation.

Figure 11.5.   Objects from the emptied room, ready to be inspected. Courtesy of Flannery O'Connor-Andalusia Foundation.

mid-twentieth century Green Stamp catalogs, farm-related brochures for machinery and equipment, and manuals for caring for livestock and domestic birds.

Getting a handle on the vast material throughout the farm involves the first steps of understanding what is there, clarifying ownership, and starting to conceive of the interpretive value of the objects. Current strategies to grow our visitation and support base include extending the visitor experience. To contribute to this engagement, we have repurposed two under-utilized rooms in the main house for programs and exhibitions. So far we have had two exhibitions that draw from materials we have found. *Test Your Mettle*, a collaboration with artists who installed some of the many metal objects we found in the Equipment Shed—from chains and tools to huge saw blades and machine parts—in an artful way that emphasized their form. The other exhibition drew from textiles found here in the house, including clothes made for Flannery by her mother, a talented seamstress. *Flannery and Fashion at Mid-Century* explores the ways in which Flannery used clothing to define her characters and also explores sewing as an historic way of life. The exhibition

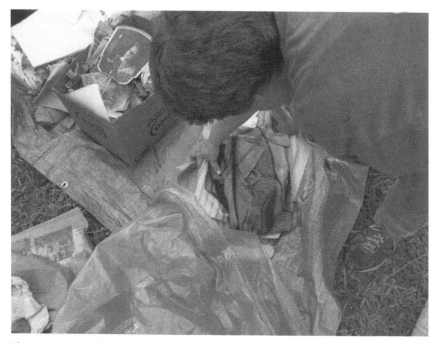

Figure 11.6. Sorting through the objects, deciding what goes to offsite storage. Courtesy of Flannery O'Connor-Andalusia Foundation.

has its own Facebook page and now has a robust life of its own beyond its six-month run in the gallery.

We have begun to plan other exhibitions that draw on the materials. We see each show as an opportunity to understand the collection needs while also making connections to the period of significance. This fosters a deeper experience for our guests both in person and on the web. The lesson is that collections can be put to work sooner rather than later. One need not wait until a complete inventory and catalog is done in order for your visitors (and you!) to learn from and about them. Similarly, the Equipment Shed rebuild is doing two things at once. We are reconstituting historic fabric while also increasing visitor services capacity with program space and restroom facilities that are handicapped accessible (doubly important at a site dedicated to a writer who used crutches and could not enter her own front door). This dual-purpose approach will continue to inform our methodology regarding the collections proper as well the buildings and landscape.

Elizabeth Wylie
Executive Director
The Flannery O'Connor Andalusia Foundation
Milledgeville, Georgia

THE ANNA MARIA ISLAND HISTORICAL SOCIETY (AMIHS)

Many local communities establish small historical societies and museums to help preserve their historical heritage. A great number of these organizations are run by volunteers who often do not have proper museum training, especially in the management of museum collections. These museums hold collections with minimal descriptive and historical information, which as a consequence, can create difficulties in future research and development.

The Anna Maria Island Historical Society (AMIHS) was one of those museums. It was created in 1992 by community members concerned with their changing community. Many of the longtime residents were moving away or passing on and rapid redevelopment of the island had begun to take place. AMIHS set out to capture this history before it disappeared, and in 1997 it also began collecting historical artifacts to help tell these stories. Over the next eighteen years it amassed more than 1,300 objects, a historic 1920s cottage, and many more archives and scrapbooks, still being processed today.

On one hot summer day in 2014, an unknown museum professional visited the museum and commented to a volunteer that they were not being good stewards to their collections. From this moment, the museum began thinking about its collections differently and initiated a relationship with a local museum consultant (this author). The consultant was initially brought in to perform a site evaluation and outline preservation concerns and list recommendations for implementation. One of the major recommendations was to complete a full inventory and catalog of the collections. Based on the recommendations, the museum chose to move forward with an inventory/catalog project.

The museum closed for a month and a half (during the slowest part of the year for tourism) to allow the consultant full access to the museum unimpeded by volunteers and patrons. The consultant set up an assembly-line type process and went room by room numbering, photographing, and taking notes in a spreadsheet. In addition, archival buffers and other preservation tools were incorporated into the displays to better protect the objects on exhibit. Over time, the process became streamlined and focused on the photography. Large sets of objects were laid out, then they were all numbered, photographed, and finally put back on display. During the photography, the consultant would place the object in a small light studio constructed of foam core and standing next to a ruler for scale and measurement. Then, the number on the object was photographed, followed by a photograph of the object itself. Once the images were uploaded to the computer, they were all easily renumbered to reflect the object number from the first photograph. This method allowed the consultant to do most of the cataloging work off-site. Armed with high-resolution photographs of the collection, the consultant could easily add measurements, descriptions, and nomenclature 3.0 vocabularies and perform web-based research.

After the collection was fully numbered and cataloged, the archives and local newspaper records were consulted for possible donor information. Since the consultant knew the collection well by the end of the cataloging, it was easier to match donor information to objects.

At the end of the project, the museum was fully cataloged, numbered, and photographed (at the project conclusion, the estimated time per object came to seven minutes each). But the question became—what do we do with all this data? A hard copy was provided to the museum for easy access, but the museum needed a computer solution that was more than just an Excel spreadsheet. The museum, however, had a number of hurdles; the critical one was that there was only one computer on-site and it spent most of its life in the closet. There was no server and no real technical support available. The museum needed an inexpensive, cloud-based, web-based solution. With these parameters, the consultant set about researching all the available open-source and web-based collections management software solutions.

The consultant put together a report on the various systems that were analyzed and included the cost and pros and cons.[1] With this report and through lengthy conversations with the museum, the choice was narrowed down to two options—eHive and Omeka. Since they were both open-source solutions, collections items were added to both possibilities and then showcased to the board of the museum. Armed with all the information, the museum chose eHive.

Once the collections management software was chosen, the museum and consultant worked with the database company to map the data into the collections database. After a short integration period of two weeks, AMIHS now had a useable, searchable museum collections database—one volunteers can easily point researchers to, as well as actively use to add new accessions and continue to incorporate complex archival data.

Ashley Burke
Collections Manager
Leepa-Rattner Museum of Art, Tarpon Springs, Florida
Museum Consultant for Burke Museum Services

ADIDAS HISTORY MANAGEMENT

We started in 2008 with about 25,000 objects, ranging from shoes to balls, product catalogs, apparel, and documents. Over time our collection grew massively, both in number and variety. As of early 2016, 57,000 objects have been cataloged, ranging from very basic to very detailed documentation with professional pictures (see www.adidas-archive.org). About the same number of uncataloged objects sit roughly sorted in our storage rooms. More than 10,000 objects that were first taken into custody were sorted out later. The collection spans over more than twenty different collection areas, and includes posters, bags, art, websites, accessories, photographs, books, and magazines.

The important part of the original collection goes back to the Adidas sports shoe museum, at the company's founding location in Herzogenaurach, Germany, which showed mainly sport shoes worn by famous athletes like Helmut Rahn, Franz Beckenbauer, Muhammad Ali, and Fritz Walter. During a restructuring process in the early 1990s the museum was closed down. Many objects were thrown away. Along with performing his other duties, an older staff member rescued many shoes from the trash, stored them in some side rooms of a factory, and took care of them. His intention was to reestablish a product library that technicians and designers could use for information and reference, as it had already existed under the company founder Adi Dassler. Conditions in these storage rooms weren't ideal. In addition to tremendous climate fluctuations, there was no protection from light or dust. At least access to the rooms was limited and objects were kept safe.

In 2008 professional museum management took over to support the planning process for a new museum. At the beginning, a museologist sorted through the collection, chose a database for cataloging, defined requirements for a new storage area, and defined first collection criteria.[2] Additional staff with collection management experience soon supported the efforts. Despite the team's good professional knowledge, establishing such a collection wasn't always easy.

Soon we realized that what was stored in the factory side rooms was not the only collection to care for. Time and time again we discover new cellars, cabinets, and boxes with interesting items—especially when older staff members retire or when departments change offices and have to clear their cellars. With the additional influx from the current range of products the number of new objects very quickly exceeded the original collection.

This constant, strong stream of new objects holds the challenge that we not only needed to develop basic structures for our collection but also that we have to constantly revise the existing collections. Many objects that we cataloged with great enthusiasm in the beginning are now on our list of possible deaccessions—for example if we since got five more of the same shoe model in considerably better condition. We could certainly handle those as new acquisitions, but for us it often feels more like we took over *one* gigantic collection that was so unorganized that we just didn't even know where all our objects were stored.

Another problem was that we only became aware of the strengths of this collection while working on it. In the beginning we just worked on what we found—for example, sports graphics or books. They seemed to be so awesome, self-contained, and easy to process topics. In retrospect we shake our heads because those objects don't fit into our mission, which is to portray the company's history and to serve as an active archive for our staff (design, legal department, and marketing). From today's point of view we would surely sort out a lot of those objects right from the start.

Maria Scherrers
Manager History Management Collection
adidas archive, Herzogenaurach, Germany

THE KENTUCKY MUSEUM

In the 1974, The Kentucky Museum had been relatively somnolent for some years. The very robust building, properly called The Kentucky Library and Museum, had been built on the campus of Western Kentucky University during the Great Depression, as a Works Progress Administration project. The library part of the building had been fairly active, with growing, important collections of archives and secondary sources pertaining to Kentucky history. The museum had largely been under the loose supervision of one man for several decades. In fact, he lived in a corner room in the lower floor of the building, surrounded by artifacts of unknown ownership. The story goes that when he was offered certain items of interest, he may have made his own decisions about whether they should enter the museum collection or become his own property.

Be that as it may, a classmate of mine in graduate school had become the museum director while I was working my way through a one-year internship. He had had the unenviable job of encouraging the old "curator" to move out, at which point I was offered the position. I visited Bowling Green, Kentucky, for interviews with the dean, department head, and others, while I in turn learned about the city and its history. It was clear that there was much to be done, with storage rooms that had been untouched in years and displays of artifacts in similar conditions. One of the exhibit "guidelines" intrigued me: "Use buff-colored index cards for display labels, since white cards tend to discolor after a few years." Actually, that was one of the few rules for anything that the director or I could find.

We were quite fortunate that the university was quite supportive of the museum at that point and we were able to set up a workshop, a clean workroom (used mostly for matting and framing and silkscreen-printing for exhibits), offices, and some new storage. The former curator's room was cleared out of the debris that he had left behind—no masterpiece art works or gold pieces, alas. That became a marshaling point for the most unmanaged items in the collections, or at least those that were not on display. We had good help in dealing with the museum's three cataloging systems, as we were able to hire about a half-dozen undergraduate students and one graduate student each semester. Needless to say, we decided to stick with the latest numbering and cataloging system, rather than create yet another layer of confusion to surround the art and artifacts. In addition, the students and the director had established a good filing system for the paper records that had previously just been stacked, in no particular order, on desks, tables, filing cabinets, and any other available surface. Our students had accomplished a good deal in inventorying those collections that were reasonably accessible, and following my arrival, we began to tackle everything else—probably about 70 percent of the collection.

Our strategy was to use our newly cleared space to sort and examine objects from shelves and boxes that had sat undisturbed for years, if not decades. The new storage furnishings were at first all constructed of Dexion slot-angle steel, with galvanized steel shelving. The material at the time was much sturdier than the current versions of it, and the shelves could hold just about any weight we might have that could be lifted by one person. We were fortunate to have a Dexion snap-cutter, which made it simple and easy to cut the steel angle to any length in one quick blow. I put together several shelf units each day for a couple of months as we made progress with the collections, and occasionally we added a special item, such as a rack for framed art works or a stand for walking sticks and canes.

The task of inventorying collections moved along in fits and starts, and our student workers did their best to reconcile our catalog cards with the objects themselves. In the process, they created a new file of ONF items (object not found), and of course as we moved ahead in each storage space we found objects with no records. Basic cataloging sheets for unrecorded items found in collection were placed in an FIC (found in collection) file. Whenever a record in the ONF file could be reunited with its artifact, it was an occasion for celebration, and it did not happen nearly as often as we would have liked. Since all our records were on paper, it was a tedious process to leaf through the catalog sheets on the off chance that a written record would match a found object. Our student workers generally felt proud to work as a team, and they felt encouraged that I worked with them, on the same tasks, to produce a proper museum record system.

On the university campus, there was help to be found at the physical plant office, with such things as adding new lights and electrical outlets here and there and painting the exhibit rooms and the new storage room. The latter actually had unfinished walls, but at least we could have the hollow tiles painted white and plan for improved accommodations in the future. Both the paint shop and carpentry shop supplied us with small, simple items as we progressed with our own projects. We even earned the grudging support of the campus locksmith, who installed new locks on the museum rooms for the first time in many years. I think he took as much pride in the improvements as we did. We were also able to take possession of used furnishings from other departments on campus, including large tables—perfect for our wood shop— and a full array of laboratory cabinets and counters for our clean workroom.

As it became possible to pick up items in storage and place them on clean shelves in a well-lighted room, we began to unearth numerous areas of unmanaged storage. One, known as "the vault" because of its solid steel door, was converted into ordinary storage, because we did not really need a vault. Aside from getting rid of the cumbersome door, we were faced with great quantities of insecticide that had been generously scattered about in previous years. It turned out that the material was a serious hazard, DDT. We were careful about cleaning up the dusty poison, but in those days the precautions one could take were not always as effective as one I might have liked. I count myself lucky that I have not developed some exotic cancer in the ensuing forty years and still keep my fingers crossed. It was indeed a happy day when the vault was clean, its old wooden shelves removed, and its concrete ceiling, walls, and floor carefully repainted. At last, we could use it as a storage space once again.

A particularly challenging storage space to conquer did not even have a name, but it was a large space filled with tall, wooden shelves, and hundreds of artifacts of all kinds in old cardboard boxes and even older, wooden, beer cases. A single, large light bulb hung in each aisle, to create an effective atmosphere of gloom. A decades-old layer of black grime covered everything. Aside from vacuuming everything that was removed from the storage room, our staff had to search countless records to match documents with objects. This was our largest storage space, but neither boxes nor shelves had any identifying numbers, and even if catalog cards included an indication of location, there were often many similar items in the same area.

In the back of that room, someone had stowed several piles of old periodicals on the floor, though most of them had become unidentifiable. In recent months, termites found their way through the concrete walls of the building, and created a colony in the heaps of paper. Needless to say, clearing out the piles of deteriorated paper and dead termites was a particularly unpleasant task.

A storage space for the art collections was found in an adjoining, smaller room. The space itself was not so dirty, and might have been a decent art storage space, but for two things: first, the framed art works were all stowed in boxes, largely without wrappings or padding of any kind; second, the room was directly above the steam pipe leading into the building, and the average temperature in the room, all year round, was close to 100 degrees, Fahrenheit. Between periods when the air was particularly humid, and the winter days when the relative humidity was close to 5 percent, the art works really suffered. In one of the first boxes we examined, we discovered a small Baroque-period painting on wood; approximately 75 percent of the paint had flaked and become detached from the wood surface, leaving us to wonder what it might have been before falling under the ministrations of the former curator.

Climate control in the museum consisted of the most elemental of controls. In some large project, years before my arrival, large window air conditioners were placed throughout the library and museum areas. Since the building systems of the 1930s could not handle the electrical load, new conduits and electrical circuits were placed on the outside walls of the building. As aesthetically displeasing as that was, we were all grateful that we had cooling and de-humidifying in the warm seasons, with at least a small degree of control over the operations. The same could not be said for the heating system; essentially, there wasn't one. The university campus had a central steam plant, and where the steam pipe entered the lower level of the library and museum building, there was a large valve, controlled by a long lever with a weight on it. The further out on the lever the weight was placed, the more steam entered the building's pipes and radiators, and for less steam, the weight could be moved closer to the inner end of the lever. Apparently, it was a new idea on our part to do anything besides allowing steam at full-bore into the pipes, and we did our best to stabilize the winter indoor temperature somewhere near seventy degrees. The results were uneven, and the protests from the older staff people in the library were bitter. Ironically, the tradition had been to produce chilly conditions inside during the summertime, and tropical heat in the winter. There seemed to be no point in trying to explain the perverseness of the situation, and so we made small changes when we could, and hoped for the best.

Over a few years, we museum staff folks were able to add quite a few archival storage furnishings for delicate collections, achieve some measure of intellectual control over the artifacts, and add one or two interpretive exhibits, as we learned more about the objects themselves. In the process, we used better exhibit methods to protect the artifacts and most certainly discarded all the buff-colored index card labels in favor of professionally produced, interpretive labels.

We worked through the state contract system to begin conservation treatments of the most important of the paintings, and set up the museum's first ongoing conservation assessment program. When the announcement was made that the museum and library building would be doubled in size with a modern addition, we felt confident that we could handle the museum operations, properly care for the collections, and make them attractive and useful to the public.

Bruce MacLeish
Curator Emeritus
Newport Restoration Foundation

THE FIDM MUSEUM AT THE FASHION
INSTITUTE OF DESIGN & MERCHANDISING

Words can't describe how excited I was to be appointed Collections Manager of the FIDM Museum at the Fashion Institute of Design & Merchandising in 2003, when I was fresh out of graduate school. My first day on the job, I remember slowly walking through one of the museum storage rooms and seeing garments hanging from bent wire hangers and yellowed plastic hangers, hats and shoes left out on open shelving—not in boxes, and old wooden filing cabinets used to hold textiles and accessories. Object tags that should have been attached to objects were scattered all over the floor amongst sequins, rhinestones, and buttons that had also fallen off. Oh, and the organization of objects wasn't entirely clear to me—other than some items were in boxes, some were hanging, and some were just sitting out in the open. To be honest, I was disappointed. It didn't look like a "real" museum to me—because I only knew about perfect museum storage as taught in graduate school. I had a lot to learn about the real world. And although I didn't know it at the time, it was going to be a tremendous learning experience to work through this collection—something that turned out to be a lot of fun and has been a very meaningful part of my career here at the FIDM Museum. And I know I am only one employee out of many who has helped make our museum a great institution.

For a bit of background, the FIDM Museum began as a small closet on the leased campus of the Fashion Institute of Design & Merchandising in the early 1970s. FIDM instructors informally founded the museum's collection. They brought vintage and designer clothing from their own wardrobes to teach students about construction techniques and fashion history. Soon, the instructors' collection packed the closet, and objects were informally "checked out" by teachers and students—much like a library. The collection

Figure 11.7.   FIDM Museum storage arranged for tours, c. 1995, Courtesy of the FIDM Museum at the Fashion Institute of Design and Merchandising, Los Angeles

grew rapidly and was physically incorporated into a room within the college library. The earliest staff who cared for the FIDM Museum collection were librarians who favored access over preservation. A former FIDM Museum & Library director was interviewed about the museum collection in 1981. She was "especially proud that the dresses, lingerie, coats, and suits—many from designers and celebrities—are accessible to students and not displayed behind glass as they are in many museums."[3] The museum's storage rooms were also used as a stop on FIDM college tours. Tour groups walked in and out of storage most days looking at the objects that were arranged more for display than preservation. At one point, accessioned shoes were even glued together and strung up on ribbons to create an eye-pleasing display.

In the late 1990s, the first staff trained in fashion history and museum management were hired. They replaced the librarians who had previously cared for the collection. They immediately embarked on a deaccession project— garments were crammed so tight on their hanging poles that it was difficult to even get a hand in to remove a single hanger. The first step toward making sense of this collection was basically getting rid of the trash—items that were badly damaged and could never be used, as well as things that were not

Figure 11.8.   FIDM Museum Storage (same view as 11.7), 2015, Courtesy of the FIDM Museum at the Fashion Institute of Design and Merchandising, Los Angeles

relevant to the collecting policy (that is, after staff developed that document). Staff also created a hands-on Study Collection, a group of objects meant to be displayed in classes and handled by students, thus promoting access and saving the rest of the collections from overhandling.

Once there was a bit more room in storage due to deaccessioning, I came on board. I asked how to purchase storage supplies and was told there had never been a designated budget, but if I came up with one, and started with the basics, that it would be approved. Easy! I ordered supplies to make padded hangers (wooden hangers covered with batting and a muslin cover) and started switching out all of the bad hangers with these good ones. At that point, I decided to arrange the hanging garments into a designated order and wrote it all down. I explained to coworkers that the Collections Manager (me) should be the only person putting objects away—once something is put away incorrectly, it's just too difficult to find again (at least until we had a computerized inventory). I also draped all the hanging garments with pre-washed muslin to prevent dust accumulation and light damage. Next, I tackled the boxed objects. We threw out the old wooden shelving and I ordered archival boxes and tissue in standard sizes because I knew that down the line that we would be planning a new compact storage system and wouldn't have the time or funds to purchase new archival supplies. This process of dealing with hanging and boxed storage took two years (we had about 12,000 objects at

Figure 11.9.   FIDM Museum accessory storage, c. 1995, Courtesy of the FIDM Museum at the Fashion Institute of Design and Merchandising, Los Angeles

this point). I found it really helpful to think of this rehousing project in terms of sections. I started at one end of the room and finished at the opposing end, but in between those two points, I worked on each section as I came across it—it felt good to be able to say something concrete, like, "I've finished hanging the wedding gowns or the Chanel Section" instead of saying, "I finished half a row and there're ten more rows to go."

As I went through the museum's collection, I saved examples of poor storage supplies (yellowed hangers, acidic tissue, yellowed boxes, old plastic garment bags that were sticky) as well as objects that had been damaged by inadequate storage and overhandling—like dresses with holes in the shoulders due to wire hangers piercing them, light-damaged items, knit garments that were stretched out due to hanging, shoes discolored from old tissue, and metallic elements tarnished from grubby hands. This is now known as our "Conservation Collection" and museum staff utilize it when we give community classes on topics like "Caring for Your Family Heirlooms" and "How to Preserve Your Wedding Gown."

The best historic fashion storage is that in which collections are hidden away. Objects hanging in covered cases or enclosed in archival boxes mean they are not exposed to light, dust, or water leaks. Researchers and non-museum staff are also less likely to "paw" through collections if they're not out in the open and they are more respectful of objects' value if staff treats them with the utmost respect. In 2007, FIDM funded a fantastic compact storage system for us. Garments and accessories are now hung or placed in boxes within metal rolling banks, and we've created covers that attach with magnets that are quite easy to remove for access. There's always room for improvement, but I feel happy now that the collection is safe and secure. And for the record, access is still a major priority for us. Instead of constant storage tours, we have a blog and a website where people can explore the collection. Researchers who would like to see individual objects just need to call or e-mail and make an appointment!

Christina M. Johnson
Associate Curator
FIDM Museum, Fashion Institute of Design & Merchandising, Los Angeles

Figure 11.10.   FIDM Museum accessory storage, 2015, Courtesy of the FIDM Museum at the Fashion Institute of Design and Merchandising, Los Angeles, CA

AN ARTIFACT MORGUE

Washington State Parks has 124 improved parks and approximately 230 total properties that it owns and/or manages. You can imagine that I, as the statewide curator of its human and natural history collections, would be hard pushed not to find something that regularly amazes me in our collections. The beginning of my string of amazing moments came just a few weeks after I was hired. I was taken to an off-site artifact storage facility in one of our parks. The park is an Army fort that was built around the turn of the twentieth century and acquired by State Parks in 1971. It contains well over a hundred buildings, structures, and fortifications, including one brick castle. Our collections were stored in the basement of the historic hospital building—which just so happens to have also been the fort morgue. And it felt like it. It was dark, cold, and dusty, as you would expect. However, it was surprisingly dry for being on a hill facing the confluence of the Strait of Juan de Fuca and Puget Sound.

There were steep stairs going down to a dimly lit corridor that passed two huge boilers and the alcoves, still pretty much as they had been, where the dearly departed would have waited processing, cleaning, and, yes, being drained of fluids. Behind a huge, metal, rolling door was another corridor that had three rooms off of it filled floor to ceiling with shelves that held historic objects and interpretive files. At the end of the corridor and behind a set of poorly hung double doors was a very large room with warehouse sized shelving filled top to bottom with more historic objects and boxes of archaeological collections. Had it not been for the rodent and insect carcasses and smell of urine and decay, my jaw would have been dragging the floor.

Over the course of the next five years, I picked away at triaging and bringing objects in to the collections facility I opened for the agency. Artifact themes were predominantly Coast Defense/Fortification and Homestead/Farming with a smattering of Civilian Conservation Corps, historic homes, and early settlement. Finds included wooden crates filled with specimens of petrified woods about 150 boxes of archaeological material, and bins, buckets, and boxes of Native American cultural material collected by the public who later abandoned them on the steps of some of our interpretive centers.

In 2012, I was told we had to empty the morgue of all artifacts. I was given a budget for additional shelving in our facility, as well as supplies and movers to help. The challenges ahead were enormous. It is always best to move objects after they've at least been assigned a number, but I didn't have time to research which park each object had originated from, nor did I have time to clean anything before it was packed. Additionally, I was a collections staff of one, which meant I had to do all of the packing myself.

Because I couldn't develop an artifact inventory using accession and catalog numbers, I created one from pictures. Temporary ID numbers based on
which room an artifact was stored in, cardinal direction that a set of shelves
were sitting in, individual shelf number, and from left to right gave each
object on the shelf a arbitrary and sequential number (i.e., A-NW-2-4, C-E-4-
10, etc.). I started by photographing each room from the doorway, then each
set of shelves followed by individual shelves, then individual objects on that
shelf. This not only allowed for the creation of a visual and written inventory,
it also allowed me to retain the original context in the event items shelved together meant something about their original location or history. I went back to
the office and created a spreadsheet using the photographs to guide me. Then,
armed with a respirator, hat, gloves, many changes of clothes and shoes, mas-
sive rolls of Ethafoam, boxes I recycled from another state agency, packing
tape, Sharpie pens, tags with strings, a flashlight, and my trusty camera, I
threw caution to all four winds and spent a week in the morgue wrapping and
packing everything I could physically carry.

I photographed every object before I wrapped it and wrote the temporary
artifact number across the packing tape. When multiple objects were put together into a box, I gave the box an arbitrary number, taped it shut on all three
sides, labeled the box with the ID number of objects enclosed, photographed
the box, and each night reviewed my photos to make notes on the master
spreadsheet as to which box objects were packed in.

Obviously, critter caresses were left behind, as were unnecessary documents, boxes of rags, and other garbage collected by well-meaning staff from
park sites. I had a pile of historic pharmaceuticals and cosmetics that I chose
to leave behind as well. Dealing with chemicals such as mercury and ammo-
nia, unlabeled glass bottles, and pest-disturbed items in compacts and tubes
was simply asking too much of my skills, so our Health and Safety Officer
was called in to properly dispose of these items.

On moving day, I had a great group of guys who could lift just about anything, but had a hard time remembering the phrases, "be careful," "be safe,"
and "slow down." Additionally, even though I had planned which objects
would go into the truck first and how we would stack things, they had other
ideas and got ahead of me. Figuring it would be best to maintain that "be careful," "be safe," frame of mind, I threw away my plans. I only cared that we
and the objects made it home in one piece. That said, there was no checking
off of items going into the trucks or later when they came off.

In one day we got the trucks loaded and made the trek back to base. The
next three days were spent double wrapping everything in clear plastic garbage bags and sealing them closed with packing tape before entering the
facility. This included items such as wheels from a Model T vehicle, coal bel-

lows over five-feet long and three-feet wide, dressers, desks, life preservers, a large grain scale, horse saddles, and so forth, and over 600 archive boxes.

I couldn't put much of the inventory through a proper freeze/thaw process so I chose to store these objects in rooms separated from general population by my office, lab and numerous doors. For the first year, daily, I inspected every plastic shrouded object, the shelves, and every inch of the three rooms to be sure there was no pest activity and I changed the pest traps more frequently than suggested. The second year I performed this close inspection a couple of times a week. It is now the third year, so I perform this inspection once a week. Coupled with the fact that I walk the entire facility and perform a cursory inspection daily, I'm comfortably confident that I can start removing the plastic from around the objects. Initially, it took me six months to check off my inventory list, but everything made it into the facility with no packing tape having been tampered with. Thankfully the most critical or fragile objects were found intact. This has left me cautiously optimistic regarding the remaining objects. Now to just figure out from which park each object originated.

Alicia Woods
Curator of Collections
Washington State Parks and Recreation Commission

NO COLLECTION IS UNMANAGEABLE!

As you have seen, tackling an unmanaged collection has its ups and downs. I sometimes compare it to a mountain hike. Almost every time it starts with a total shock and the overwhelming feeling that there is no way this collection will ever begin to somehow resemble a proper museum collection. You feel much like when you're standing at the bottom of a mountain and can't see the summit because it's high up in the clouds. But as you roll up your sleeves and start working with the collection, you suddenly realize things start to change and there's progress. You reach the first logical exits, just as you reach the first lookout points and see that you actually advanced. When you don't get funding for appropriate storage furniture or you discover that there's mold, you feel devastated and helpless again, just as you do when you discover that a landslide has destroyed the hiking path. Then, you pull yourself up by your own bootstraps and keep on working, just as you do when you decide to climb a few meters or discovered a different path to bypass the landslide. Sometimes, the only thing that saves your day is thinking about the moment you can do your diary entry and call it a day, just as thinking about the next tea/snack break keeps you walking. The longer you work with the collection, the less you notice improvements. It may take a special occasion to let you see that you've come a long way, like the moment you turn around a corner and suddenly see how near you are to the summit. Maybe it is when the first pallet of archival boxes arrives. Maybe it is when you realize that now, for the first time, you can walk down all the aisles without falling over an object that has been stored there. Maybe it is when a colleague who knows what the collection was like five years ago comes visiting and expresses her surprise and respect for your achievements. For me it was when a colleague with whom I worked side-by-side for a long time and who taught me everything about craning heavy machinery (and to use brains instead of brawn, which probably saved my back a couple of times) stated that, in his opinion, the storage of the TECHNOSEUM had become "too tidy for the storage of a science and technology museum." It was an enlightening moment. It was the moment I realized that, while there is still a lot of work to do and the collection is far from how I want it to be stored and managed, there really is visible improvement. And, in the words of Alicia Woods, "As long as we take no steps backward— I can keep moving forward."[4] Take these words of encouragement and keep the mountain hike in mind as you start working on your collection.

In the beginning, I promised with this book to give you a road map to follow when you are tackling your own unmanaged collection. I hope I gave you a good one. You will have to adapt it to your circumstances. Every situation and every collection is different and deserves plans and solutions that are especially tailored to this need. Your collection might be in such good shape that you can skip a few steps, which will certainly be the case if you just have to include an unmanaged collection into an existing, well-managed one. You might run into difficulties I never encountered and couldn't even think of. You might find that some of the recommendations given in this book, or in fact the whole professional literature, may not be applicable in your case. The logical exits I suggested should work in most cases, but maybe your case is so special you have to define yours in another way. But, definitely, make sure you define logical exits! You always need a goal toward which you can work, otherwise you get lost in all the work involved with a collection. I hope all the real-world examples convinced you that no collection is unmanageable, no matter how bad the situation seemed to be in the beginning. And I hope the chapters gave you an idea of how you can define and achieve your goals.

It's your collection and it's your path. Make sure your path is safe to travel and may the road rise to meet you!

NOTES

1. The report can be found on http://world.museumsprojekte.de/wp-content/uploads/2015/07/Review-of-affordable-Collections-Database-options.pdf

2. "Museologist" is a term used for the German job title "Museologe." This normally indicates someone who has graduated in Museum Studies and covers a wide range of different job responsibilities from collections manager to exhibition coordinator, as needed and defined by the museum or institution.

3. "The Private Eyes of Fashion," *Los Angeles Times*, April 25, 1981.

4. Alicia Woods, e-mail to the author, March 30, 2015.

Bibliography

The shed is full of objects, the roof is leaking, and I'm not sure if there is any documentation about this collection—do I really have time to read? I know that feeling. But in order to do the right thing, you have to know what the right thing is and how to do it. Even if you have a museum studies degree and years of experience in collections management under your belt, there are still some resources you should have at hand for reference. Throughout the book I tried to avoid doubling up with information you can find in more detail elsewhere. I pointed to those references in the text, so here, in the bibliography I will repeat the references I think you will need no matter what type of collection you deal with.

This also means that this bibliography represents a minimum. You will have to look into more resources that fit the special need of your collection, like handling, storage, and conservation guides for certain materials, or when it comes to cataloging, history books, magazines, and mailing catalogs. I tried to sort the resources by the stage in your project you will need them.

BEFORE YOU START

You are probably eager to start right here and now, but before you do that, you should definitely read through these two books:

Catlin-Legutko, Cinnamon, and Stacy Klingler. *Stewardship: Collections and Historic Preservation.* Book 6, *Small Museum Toolkit.* Lanham, MD: AltaMira Press, 2012.

Reibel, Daniel B.: *Registration Methods for the Small Museum.* Lanham, MD: AltaMira Press, 2008.

These books are both of reasonable length and good to read.

Even if your collection is not in an industrial building, the following book sharpens your senses on what to look for in the building your collection is stored in:

Bordass, Bill. *Museum Collections in Industrial Buildings: A Selection and Adaptation Guide.* London: Museums and Galleries Commission, 1996.

There's one more book, but unfortunately it is long out of print. However, if you manage to get a copy, definitely read this:

Stuckert, Caroline M. *Cataloging from Scratch. A Manual for Cataloging Undocumented Collections in Small Museums.* Havertown, PA: MACC Associates, 1991.

These books will prepare you with basic background knowledge of working processes in museum collections, although they can't replace thorough training and years of experience in the field.

AT YOUR DESK

While the books of the last section were meant to be read through, there are some other books that should sit on your desk as references, so you can look up the relevant passages when you need them. Those are the following:

Buck, Rebecca A., and Jean Allmann Gilmore. *Museum Registration Methods.* 5th ed. (MRM5). Washington, DC: The AAM Press, 2010.

Dawson, Alex, and Susanna Hillhouse, eds. *SPECTRUM 4.0.* London: Collections Trust, 2011. It is available to download free for registered users and noncommercial use at http://www.collectionstrust.org.uk/spectrum/spectrum-homepage.

Malaro, Marie C., and Ildiko P. DeAngelis. *A Legal Primer on Managing Museum Collections.* Washington, DC: Smithsonian Books, 2012.

NPS Museum Handbook, Parts I–III. Washington, DC: National Park Service, 1984ff. You'll find the most up-to-date version on the website of the National Park Services (http://www.nps.gov/), where you can download it as a whole or in single chapters for free.

National Trust. *The National Trust Manual of Housekeeping: Care and Conservation of Collections in Historic Houses.* Oxford: Butterworth-Heinemann, 2005.

Southeastern Registrars Association, ed. *Basic Condition Reporting. A Handbook.* Lanham, MD: Rowman & Littlefield Publishers, 2015.

WHILE WORKING

While the books in the previous section should definitely be at hand anytime (if possible), the following books are helpful at some steps during the working process. When you are laying out your collections plan, writing your collections policy, and developing procedures of how your collection is used, the following resources are helpful:

Gardener, James B., and Elizabeth E. Merrit. *The AAM Guide to Collections Planning.* Washington, DC: AAM Press, 2004.
Simmons, John E. *Things Great and Small: Collections Management Policies.* Washington, DC: AAM Press, 2006.

When you start accessioning and cataloging your collection the following resources will be helpful in addition to those already mentioned:

Bourcier, Paul, Ruby Rogers, and the Nomenclature Taskforce, eds. *Nomenclature 4.0 for Museum Cataloging. Robert G. Chenhall's System for Classifying Cultural Objects.* Lanham, MD: AltaMira Press, 2010.
Buck, Rebecca A., and Jean A. Gilmore, eds. *Collection Conundrums: Solving Collections Management Mysteries.* Washington, DC: AAM Press, 2007.

When you come to storage planning look into the following:

Dawson, Alex, ed. *Benchmarks in Collections Care for Museums, Archives and Libraries.* London: Museums, Archives and Libraries Council, 2011.
Lord, Barry, Gail Dexter Lord, and Lindsay Martin. *Manual of Museum Planning: Sustainable Space, Facilities, and Operations,* Lanham, MD: AltaMira Press, 2012.
Cultural Heritage Division of UNESCO, ed. *Methodology and Didactic Tools for Re-Organizing Museum Storage,* 2009, http://unesdoc.unesco.org/images/0018/001862/186244e.pdf.

WEB RESOURCES

There are hundreds of good resources on the web, but it's also a big black hole in which your time disappears. Here are a few starting points for research and thought exchange on special issues that might serve your purpose better than hitting keywords into the next search engine:

Connecting to Collections Care: An online community, powered by the American Institute for Conservation and the Institute of Museum and Library Services, that provides both resources and an active discussion platform: http://www.connecting-tocollections.org/.

Conserv O Grams of the National Park Service: a collection of information on the handling and storage of various materials: http://www.nps.gov/museum/publications/conserveogram/cons_toc.html.

Registrars Committee of the American Alliance of Museums (RC-AAM): RC-AAM has a couple of resources on its website, but it especially has a very helpful listserv to post questions and conundrums to: http://www.rcaam.org/Listserv.

Index

About the Author

Angela Kipp is currently the collections manager of the TECHNOSEUM in Mannheim, Germany, and an independent museum consultant. She graduated as a Diplom-Museologin (FH) in Museum Studies from the Fachhochschule für Technik und Wirtschaft (University of Applied Sciences) in Berlin. Starting off as a travelling database troubleshooter and project assistant for various exhibitions, Kipp has worked in the museum field since 1998 for museums of all sizes. Since then she has seen, worked for, and advised about many unmanaged or only partly managed collections. Since 2004 Kipp has overseen the collection of the TECHNOSEUM, one of the three largest science and technology museums in Germany, with about 170,000 objects.

Angela Kipp's special focus includes historical, technological, and agricultural collections; project management, logistics, the purposeful use of technology and media in the museum context, and interdisciplinary teamwork. In 2013 she cofounded "Registrar Trek—The Next Generation," a volunteer-run blog that fosters the exchange between collections professionals around the world by publishing and translating articles, stories, and practical advice about collections care.